Informative and provocative! Don't s
this first. Clare Norman's book offer
derailers that can serve to lessen the
experience of how the coach, client ... ... ...............ii can be
more deliberate in how they choose, use and leverage coaching in
order to maximise personal and business impact.

**Michelle Lucas – master executive coach and master coach
supervisor, Greenfields Consulting Ltd**

A revelation that broadens our understanding of partnership
and challenges us to consider the readiness of our clients. Clare
Norman has a unique gift for understanding the true needs of
the coaching profession. Her approach uncovers the authentic
elements coaches need to recognise to embrace the right and
ready clients. Our coaching skills are not enough if they can't be
used in the best contexts.

**Matthew Cintron-Quiñones, MCC, BCC**

This book delves deep into the essential concept of coaching
readiness by shifting the responsibility for value creation from the
coach to the thinker and underscoring the need for thinkers to
develop accountability and self-efficacy.

**Mel Leow, MCC – leadership coach, speaker and author of**
*Engage: How to stop living in default and start living the life
you desire*

I am overjoyed that Clare Norman has written this book. I wish
I had access to this book when I first started out as a coach and
still, after many years of coaching, I gleaned lots of ideas that I am
excited to integrate into my own coaching practice. It is an easy-
to-read book and provides structure, templates and questions for
both coaches and coaching custodians in organisations that will
guide them in how best to ensure there is coaching readiness by
all parties engaging in the coaching process.

**Ailbhe Harrington MA, MCC – executive coach, coach
supervisor, director of education, Aspire Coach Training**

From well before the compatibility session to the last meeting, this is a groundbreaking roadmap for coaches. When I began reading this book, my initial thought was, 'Where has this information been all my coaching life?' My excitement grew as I realised just how profound and vitally important this is for all coaches, both internal and external.

> **Gail Moore, CPC – creator and host,** *Inside the World of Master Coaching*

This is a must-read book and should be required reading for every coach who aspires to partner effectively with thinkers who are looking for agency and sustainable and authentic change. Clare Norman addresses every nook and cranny of the coaching experience.

> **Roger Fielding, MCC, mentor coach and course tutor, Cambridge University coaching programmes**

A practical and insightful resource that guides coaches to play a more powerful role and become even more effective with the people they work with. Beneficial for both coaches and organisations utilising coaching services, this guide is a valuable contribution for anyone committed to impactful coaching and for those who seek to engage in meaningful work with clients beyond just commercial considerations.

> **Karen White, MCC – director of training and course leader, Ontological Coaching Institute**

Clare Norman offers practical tools, methodologies, processes and powerful reflections which can be seamlessly integrated into coaching practices, fostering a deeper understanding of client needs and expectations. It challenges existing paradigms and offers fresh perspectives, making it a must-read for anyone committed to excellence in coaching.

> **Marie Quigley, MCC – director, Empower World**

# Cultivating Coachability

How to leverage coaching readiness
so thinkers can optimise value

By the bestselling author of *The Transformational Coach*

## CLARE NORMAN, MCC

with Dr Sam Humphrey

**Cultivating Coachability**
ISBN 978-1-915483-49-2 (paperback)
ISBN 978-1-915483-50-8 (ebook)

Published in 2024 by Right Book Press
Printed in the UK

A CIP record of this book is available from the British Library.

# Contents

# Foreword

Witnessing clients making changes, stretching outside of their comfort zone, delivering impact in their lives, organisations and communities is one of my greatest joys as a coach.

If my greatest joy comes from my clients' successes, conversely my biggest frustration comes from working with people who have no readiness to develop and grow. A client sent to me via a third party recently told me: 'I'm exhausted doing all this thinking. Can't you pick the topic for the next session and tell me what to do?' It would be akin to an athlete asking their coach to run the race for them.

The coach doesn't run the race. The athlete does.

We shouldn't jump to judgement though. Many people simply don't know what coaching is nor how different it is from any other conversation. Once they understand how to make the most of it, they may turn out to become your best client ever!

This is where the concept of coachability and Clare's book comes in. Coaching has to be the 'right' intervention at the 'right' time, with a client 'right and ready' for coaching and with the 'right' support from their organisation.

In her book, Clare generously provides clear checklists and resources that coaches can apply to their practice right away to make sure the organisation plays its part and that the client puts in the work and turns up at their best.

The book walks us through each step of the journey, from before the coach and client start their work together through to completion. The set-up of coaching readiness is vital and where the client is not self-funding, that starts with the commissioning organisation, associate company or coaching platform.

The simple (though perhaps not always easy) act of fostering coaching readiness and coachability in our clients *and* their environment enables clients to take responsibility for their own thinking.

This touches on a bigger dimension. Let me explain...

Coaches encourage clients to explore uncomfortable places – such as prejudice, judgement, limiting beliefs or shame.

As they take responsibility for their thinking and doing, our clients experience new-found agency and behave differently in their environment.

A client of mine was exploring tensions within a multicultural team he was leading. Through the coaching, he realised how his judgement around team members' religious practices was impacting his ability to constructively engage with them. He started the session by telling me how the team members were behaving in unacceptable ways. Suddenly, he stopped talking mid-sentence and sighed. 'I have a lot of work to do,' he said. He realised that to be able to truly engage with his team members, he first needed to develop empathy and understanding for their needs. This was a breakthrough moment in our session.

My favourite moment came a few seconds later though. My client stayed quiet and then said, 'We could solve many conflicts in the world if we approached them in this way.'

By emphasising coachability, we help our clients develop agency. This process has ripple effects way beyond the immediate coaching context. The coach–client relationship becomes a blueprint for possible behaviour in the client's other relationships and their broader environment. They behave differently in the world and inspire others to develop agency, too. With the complex issues our world is facing, it seems to me that this is a wonderful gift.

Thank you, Clare, for articulating it in simple terms and making it accessible to us.

**Lise Bruynooghe**
Master Certified Coach, coach supervisor, president, UK ICF

# Introduction

## Creating value in coaching

Your job as coach is *not* to create value. **Your job is to be a catalyst for the creation of value, but not to create value yourself.**

This book is about shifting where value is created in coaching – shifting the responsibility for value creation to the thinker.

Your responsibility as a coach is to take care of the process so that the thinker (see below) can create that value themselves, enabling them to access their inner wisdom, connect their own dots and find answers that match their personality, context, motivations, beliefs and values.

Therefore the thinker needs to be ready and willing to take that responsibility for creating value. In other words, they need to be 'coaching ready'. They need to have some agency, some self-efficacy – although, of course, coaching can also support them to build agency and self-efficacy along the way.

By agency, I mean self-determination – a sense of control over one's choices rather than handing power over to someone else; the willingness to think for oneself, to make decisions and act in accordance with those decisions – intentionality, if you like. Bandura (2006) describes those with agency as 'producers of their life circumstances and not just the products of them'. And yes, this builds over the course of coaching but thinkers need some agency to build upon as they come into coaching.

And by self-efficacy, I mean one's belief in one's own ability to change and grow. Again, this can be built on over the course of coaching, but it's an important input to the process.

I recognise that our educational systems haven't necessarily done the best job of setting up people for a life of agency, so some may need more support and challenge than others to embrace the idea that change comes from within, not from without.

Moving away from the mindset that it's your role to create

value and towards a belief that it's the thinker's role might be quite a shift for you. Beliefs drive behaviours, so updating your beliefs precedes taking action that matches those beliefs, in this case around where value is created. I hope to support you in this book through that mindset reset.

## Who is the thinker?

If you haven't read my companion book, *The Transformational Coach* (2022), you may already have been stopped in your tracks by the portrayal of a person who comes to coaching as the thinker. This is what they're there to do – to *think* for themselves. The term comes from Nancy Kline's (2002) work around the Thinking Environment. It's beyond the scope of this book to write about the components that make up the Thinking Environment, but I will say that Nancy's work has been influential in my own development as a coach.

In *The Transformational Coach* and this book, my focus is on one-to-one coaching. You may find useful input for group or team coaching, but there will be additional things to pay attention to when deciding whether a group or team is coaching ready and how to enhance their coachability and agency. That's beyond the scope of this book, so I'd point you to Georgina Woudstra and Allard de Jong at Team Coaching Studio for more insights into that area (see Woudstra 2021).

**Your job as one-to-one coach is to provide a learning laboratory through all that you do and all that you say to build the thinking muscles of the thinker.**

They may not (yet) trust their own thinking and may not know what it means to think well, but you can hold fast to the belief that they can and will think well, given the chance.

Your job is *not* to do the thinking for them, no matter how developed (or not) their thinking muscles are. It's not to join the dots that you're seeing, but rather to ask them to join the dots between the things they've said, as they'll likely join a different set of dots that has more meaning to them and their situation.

Just as a personal trainer doesn't lift weights to enable you to build physical muscles, the coach doesn't lift thinking weights to enable the thinker to build their thinking muscles. The personal trainer and the coach each provide the environment and encouragement for the other person to build their own physical, or in this case, thinking muscles.

But the word thinker doesn't encompass everything I'd like it to cover. Your role as coach is not only to tap into their intellectual thinking, but also to extract the wisdom that their feelings and emotions convey to them; to use their somatic sensing to find new meaning; to access other forms of intelligence such as the visual, kinaesthetic, auditory – not to mention finding insight through nature's metaphors.

'Seldom do we teach the skills of thinking, feeling and being, which are inputs to everything we conceive, believe and behave,' writes Tim Rogers (2022). All of this is part of cultivating coaching readiness – enabling the thinker to think, feel and be so that they can conceive, believe and behave in ways that are (more) useful to them.

Perhaps you might call the thinker the explorer or the senser. Certainly, they're the pilot or the driver of their own life, but what comes first, before flying or driving to somewhere new? Thinking – and being a self-directed learner. According to Koch and Gittleson (2013), high-performance learners are self-directed and:

* take responsibility for managing their time, completing their work and planning their learning experiences
* are proactive about seeking regular detailed feedback from multiple sources, and then act upon it
* are intentional when planning the learning opportunities required to get to where they want to be
* stretch themselves with new roles or responsibilities – practical experiences that will speed their development
* network and join forces to solve their and others' problems

* are agile and flexible regarding their development, and responsive to learning needs that arise
* are future oriented, knowing what role they want next in their career.

While not everyone who comes to coaching is as self-directed as this, you can support and challenge them through the coaching to embrace these traits, which map to what you might know as coachability.

I see coaching readiness and coachability as similar but not exactly interchangeable. Coaching readiness is setting the coaching up for success from the start, pre-coaching; coachability is within coaching. But I am jumping ahead slightly. We'll come back to definitions in a while.

## My purpose as a master coach, master mentor coach, coach supervisor and human

I'm here to make (organisational) life more human, one thinker or team at a time. I want to contribute to a world that fights less and loves more. You may also be in the business of making life more human, one thinker or team at a time. In that endeavour, I'm committed to your uniqueness as a coach. You are like no other coach out there. And the thinkers with whom you work are like no other thinkers out there. They too are unique.

I'm committed to high-quality coaching and have an eye for detail when it comes to the language you use – language that enables the thinker to become an independent, critical decision maker. Taking the lead from Formula 1 and world-class cycling, where every second counts, I'm constantly on the lookout for marginal gains in coaching. Not to shave off time (although in some instances, it could be to give maximum time to the thinker to think); instead, to create the best Thinking Environment for them so they can do their best thinking. Everything that coaches do or say can have an impact on the thinker's coaching readiness and therefore their capacity to think.

I also notice how much my coaching is informed by agency. This has been a theme for me over the years, but only now am I joining the dots in relation to it. There's my own agency: my desire to be independent, self-sufficient, driven and successful in my own way. I hate the thought of giving away my agency. And because I hate that thought, I want to be sure that others don't give away their agency either.

I'm starting to realise how intertwined coachability/coaching readiness and agency are and why it really matters to me to get this book into others' hands.

**My 'why' is for everyone to find their voice, to articulate their needs, to stand up for themselves.**

I don't always do that for myself, and I know how hard it can be, but it's so important to express what we feel and what needs are associated with those feelings. In his book, *Nonviolent Communication* (2003), Marshall Rosenberg explains how he has seen this lead to better negotiations, reducing the propensity to resort to violence. That's why agency and expressing oneself are so important to me, for a more peaceful world.

# Why am I writing this book?

I'm driven to innovate, to think afresh, to be a bit edgy and provocative. You might experience that provocation as you read this book. At the same time, I have some angst about naming what I see. What will people think of me? Must I have it all figured out? But there it is, my human fragility, front and centre. You can judge me if you wish, but I would prefer you to use this book to provoke your own thinking around this sometimes emotive subject of coaching readiness, coachability and agency.

I've noticed that coach training companies teach people to coach. No surprise there, you might think. But what I've come to realise is that this focuses on the coaching session. Again, no surprise there. I'm all for that focus on how you coach, not how you talk about your coaching. That's why I endorse and invest in mentor coaching (observed coaching using a benchmark set of competencies to give feedback).

But what about all the other parts of the coaching experience? Not the sales and marketing aspects, but the thinker's experience. Where does a coach learn about all of that? And not just the programme of coaching itself, which the coach has control over, but also the essential wraparound parts of the experience, which involve other stakeholders, particularly in organisational coaching conducts. What you'll read here about the elements of the end-to-end experience is underpinned by the International Coaching Federation (ICF) Code of Ethics.

Alongside internal and external coaching experience, I have a background in human-centred design. That means putting the human at the centre of how we design products and experiences, in this case putting the thinker at the centre of the coaching experience. You might call this 'experience design for thinking'. That's why I'll cover the whole coaching experience in this book.

It's not all up to the coach to draw out coaching readiness. **This is an end-to-end experience that we're designing here.**

There are many other stakeholders involved in this experience: for example, the coaching custodian in an organisation, the sponsor, peer support. I'll be highlighting their roles in coaching readiness as well as the roles within the dyad of coach and thinker, who don't operate in isolation.

I'm fascinated by this idea of coaching readiness and have been exploring the coaching experience through that lens. Coachability was a term I heard frequently about 15–20 years ago, but it seems to have died away, even though coaches' frustrations with it have not. Now that I've been coaching for more than 20 years, I wanted to revisit what I prefer to call coaching readiness through a more experienced lens but still with a beginner's mindset.

As T S Eliot wrote in 1942, 'We must not cease from exploration, and the end of all our exploring will be to arrive where we began and to know the place for the first time.' This book is a product of my continued exploration of coaching readiness and agency, an exploration that I suspect will never cease. As I said, it's a book that I hope will provoke you to think for yourself, not necessarily to take my word for it. It's an invitation to think with me. None of us has the definitive answers to anything in this complex world of ours. But this is the way I see things today, as I write. My thinking will no doubt evolve well after the book goes to print.

I don't pretend to have all the answers. That's the 'tyranny of the together coach' (a phrase shared with me by my current coaching supervisor, Simon Cavicchia), who feels they need to have it all figured out. I'm not falling for that! And much of what I've learned comes from others who have come before me, many of whom I will quote, where I know where the insights emanated from. I hope to have distilled some useful information here, practical applications that will enable you to draw out the best thinking from those you coach. You can then take your own wonderings to supervision, to enhance your own skills in screening for and enhancing coaching readiness and coachability.

I see this book as the prequel to *The Transformational Coach,* in which I say that coaching is a joint endeavour, a partnership. So how do you enable the thinker to fully inhabit the role of partner rather than consumer? All of your masterful coaching only works if you focus on their coaching readiness as well as your own.

That coaching readiness isn't necessarily innate. If the thinker has never experienced coaching before, or if they've had a different form of coaching to that which you offer, they'll come to coaching in a naïve and innocent state about what it is and how to get the most from it. You know much more than they do about how the *process* of coaching works, so it's up to you – and other stakeholders in this whole experience – to open their eyes to the potential of coaching, should they choose to embark wholeheartedly on an exploration of who they are and what's most meaningful to them.

In my experience, coaches work too hard to create value. It's not your role to provide value; rather it's the thinker's role to extract value with your support and challenge and the other stakeholders' roles to provide the environment within which the thinker can maximise that value. **I do want thinkers to walk away with value from their coaching, but not to the extent that I'll do the thinking for them.**

If you haven't done so already, I encourage you to read or listen to *The Transformational Coach* to understand the mindsets that *you* need to unlearn to be a more masterful coach, such as not trying so hard. This book that you have in your hands is about the mindsets we can encourage *thinkers* to unlearn and replace with more coaching-ready mindsets. But start with yourself first. *And* be more demanding of the other stakeholders in the process too. I hope this book might enable you to influence a better set-up of coaching programmes when they're organisationally funded and to create a better foundation when the coaching is individually funded.

I've found myself getting more and more interested in the role that context plays in coaching. My job is to support and challenge people to think rather than toe the party line, and it's not to collude with the system that's paying me. It's time to rail against the efficiency paradigm that goes on in organisations and hold them to account for effective coaching. That's their job as well as mine. My intention is to invite you to consider what goes on in the commissioning of coaching and define your own requests of them for more effective coaching to take place. I invite you to test out and experiment with what I offer here, being brave in some cases by requiring more upfront preparation by others.

Please remember that this is a snapshot of my thinking as it stands today, and you'll be able to build on it by discussing with peers and your supervisor and by testing things out in your own world. In the course of writing the book, I became aware of the tension we as coaches put on ourselves for 'ten-step programmes' and the 'one right way': some of what I write about here, though, is new territory (for me at least), so how we navigate this territory is a work in progress. There's no one right way, which is why supervision is invaluable for exploratory purposes rather than black-and-white answers.

# The key mindsets I encourage you to embrace when reading this book

It may help you to understand the mindsets that influence me as I write this book. You may or may not hold these same beliefs. I encourage you to consider these now, though, so that you understand where the content is coming from. Please don't skim over these; pay them some attention, be curious, maybe even take them to supervision to ponder.

✳ As coaches, we're working with human beings (I don't think you can really argue with this one!).

✳ There are many other stakeholders who have a role to play in enhancing coaching readiness.

✳ I can plant seeds at every step of the coaching experience that encourage greater agency in the thinker and therefore value creation.

✳ The thinker is 'creative, resourceful and whole' (Whitworth et al 1998) and therefore they're perfectly capable of creating that value.

✳ Coaching is a partnership, and it requires intentional practice from both parties.

✳ My responsibility is to encourage and enhance the thinker's thinking and learning for themselves. Their responsibility is to wring the most value out of the coaching.

✳ Coaching isn't just another meeting; it's self-development, so the rules of engagement are entirely different.

✳ Coaching is also not a cosy chat. It's a place for challenge and stepping up. It's not to be taken lightly.

✳ Stop and think at every step of the coaching experience: are you setting up this coaching for learning?

**'The promise of stretching is not success, it's learning. It's self-insight. It's the promise of gleaning answers to some of the most important and vexing questions of our lives: What do we want? What can we do? Who can we be?'** (Heath & Heath 2017).

✳ Come to coaching with a beginner's mind – you may be an expert in the process, but you're not an expert in the thinker's solutions. Get comfortable with not knowing.
✳ We all have choice.
✳ Relationship is key, and relationships are complex and intricate.

As I contemplate these beliefs, I see non-directive coaching reflected back at me. This is where I tend to spend my time as a coach. Bartolome et al (2022) define non-directive coaching as 'non-transference of knowledge or experience' and 'non-issuance of judgements by the coach'. That's where I place myself on the coaching spectrum, though it hasn't been a straightforward path to get here. It has taken a lot of supervision, mentor coaching and reflective practice to get used to not having answers.

I'm sharing all of this because it informs everything you're about to read.

## Introducing Dr Sam Humphrey

You'll notice that Sam Humphrey and I have co-written some of the content. She and I were reintroduced to each other in 2023 when Sam was recording her podcast *Coaching Stories*. I was one of her guests. The podcast is based on her book with Karen Dean, *Coaching Stories: Flowing and Falling of Being a Coach* (2019). Flowing stories are those where the coach has been in flow; falling stories recognise that none of us are perfect. My flowing story alluded to coachability. The person I was working with presented with agency.

⭐ It was a coaching demonstration, in front of a group of coaches, just after I had received my Master Certified Coach (MCC) credential. It can be tricky working with someone with whom you have no prior relationship, as you don't know how they'll present nor what their thinking style is. I also felt a little more pressure to be masterful due to having just received that designation of MCC.

But in this particular demonstration, we'd been talking with the group beforehand about tapping into multiple intelligences through creative means (see Shift 72 in *The Transformational Coach*). As soon as the thinker and I started coaching, she said she was really excited to experiment and find new ways to process her issue. So I took that as an invitation to be courageous in our work together, not holding back anything that my intuition brought forth. It was one of the best demonstrations I've ever co-created with a thinker.

Why? It wasn't about my courage, it was about hers. She was willing. She wanted to be challenged. She was up for change. She was curious.

My worst falling stories have been with people who didn't want to think for themselves and I ignored my instincts about whether I should work with them. I'll write about a few of them throughout the book. I'm not proud of these case studies and I don't always get it right today, but the stories will give you some hints about what can go wrong if you ignore the warning signs.

As a result of discussing these stories, Sam and I got excited about the possibility of exploring coachability further together as a determinant of return on expectations in coaching. I'd already put a proposal forward to my publisher and asked Sam whether she'd like to come on board, particularly in the sections that are about the coaching custodian's role because it's a role that she held in Unilever and her experiences at that time profoundly informed her work as a coach. And the rest is history. What a wise decision to write together, for all that we originated together.

Here's Sam's motivation for being a part of this endeavour:

*I've reached a stage in my coaching career where I've been doing it for so long that I forget how much I know. The coaching landscape is so very different to when I first dipped my toe in this water and, as with any evolution, things get lost or forgotten. Coachability is one of those things. Of late, I've often found myself sat in front of a potential coaching client who has a coaching goal, knows what they need to do to achieve it, yet has little motivation, energy or willingness to take action. As a professional coach, I think it's bordering on unethical for me to work with this client, as I know that no matter how good a coach I am – and sometimes I think I am rather good – if the client isn't willing to take action, experiment or shift, nothing will change. The podcast gods sent Clare to me at the right time as it led to us collaborating on this book. It's a vehicle for me to share my knowledge and experience in a constructive way and its publication may also lead to more robust practices around coachability. It would be a real treat to know that this book might effect changes that mean my fellow coaches only sit in front of clients for whom coaching is a good fit at that time.*

## How to use this book for continuous professional development

I'd like to think that you might feel relieved as you read this book. You're not the only one who encounters frustration or other emotions when the thinker with whom you're working doesn't invest in the work. I hope you'll walk away feeling a sense of your own agency. Yes, there *are* things that you and your stakeholders can do or say at every step of the way to enhance the coaching readiness of thinkers.

I invite you to recognise your own values in this space and set your own (perhaps negotiable, but never demolish-able) boundaries for whom you work with and how.

I've attempted to structure the book in bite-sized chunks so that you can read a page or two and put the book down to digest what you've read.

I also encourage you to put the book down after each chapter and practise what you've learned. Bite-sized, spaced practice will help you to cement the learning (Brown et al 2014) before moving on to the next section and committing to more bite-sized, spaced practice and building layer upon layer of higher-value coaching. But please don't feel that you're alone in your reflective practice. Take your questions, concerns, tensions and paradoxes to supervision. That may be one to one, or it may be in a group, where you'll hear other coaches tussling with similar questions, concerns, tensions and paradoxes.

A work-related book is only as good as the changes you make as a result of reading it. I can't make you change, but I hope that you'll read with a view to updating your process around coaching readiness. To that end, I'll invite you into reflective practice at the end of each chapter, asking questions such as:

❊  What do *you* believe about this?
❊  Which of your values are showing up?
❊  What will you ask for and from whom? Which of these boundaries are non-negotiable and in which circumstances might you flex?
❊  What's the one thing you commit to experiment with that will make a marginal gain in the coaching readiness of the people with whom you work?

Please don't gloss over these reflective practice elements. If you do, you'll be doing yourself and the thinkers with whom you work a disservice because you'll forget much of what you've read and not make changes. If you keep a continuous professional development journal, perhaps you might write your notes there.

Please approach the book with a growth mindset (Dweck 2017). A fixed mindset would constitute doing as I say, ticking things off your list. A growth mindset is much more about becoming the best coach *you* can be, given your personality, beliefs, values and motivations.

I include many case studies (shown with a ✪), resources, checklists, questionnaires, templates. Please feel free to steal anything marked by a downward arrow (⬇) with pride, but adapt them to match your style, beliefs, values and motivations. If you would like editable versions of these resources, you can download them at **clarenormancoachingassociates.com/cultivating-coachability/templates/** and use the code **ValueCreation**.

Experiment with these resources. Play. Fail and learn. As ex-media CEO turned author Margaret Heffernan (2020) writes: 'The great advantage of experiments is that they stop you being stuck; they're one way to prototype the future.'

I say again, as I also wrote in *The Transformational Coach*: experiment, play, fail and learn. And then reward yourself! That immediate reward will entice you to repeat or enhance the experiment.

Hard is good when it comes to trying out new ways of being and doing things (Brown et al 2014). I encourage you not to give up, but to put in the emotional investment to make changes. As I mentioned previously, work with a supervisor to get feedback from outside yourself. And with that, enjoy the learning and the challenge. If you want further reading, all of the references are in the Bibliography – but read this book and *The Transformational Coach* first! And put the experiments into practice. Integration into your practice is key.

# How to navigate the book

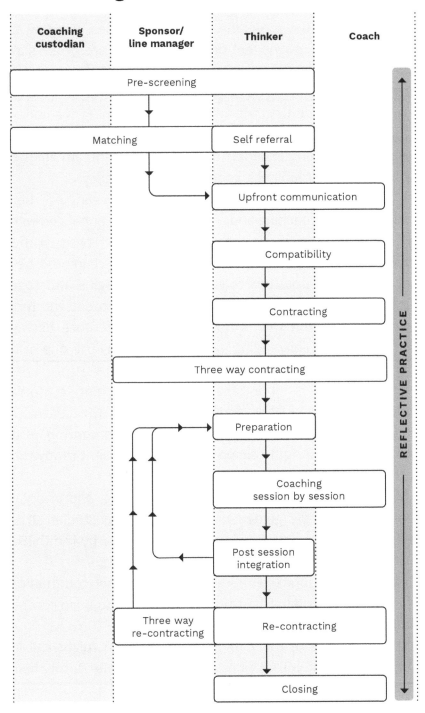

On the previous page is the experience diagram that the book will take you through, in the chronological order of the coaching experience from pre-screening to close. At times, bringing this experience to life might feel difficult as there are other stakeholders to influence. But it'll be worth it for the difference it makes, when each thinker is willing to take the steering wheel.

I'll set the scene first, introducing why coaching readiness is important, what it is and how to spot it. And then we'll delve into designing a coaching experience that taps into and amplifies the traits of coaching readiness, coachability and agency.

I alluded earlier to the idea of coaching readiness being screened for pre-coaching and coachability being enhanced within coaching. You'll see in the contents page how I have split these across the coaching experience, with coaching readiness being front and centre until the coaching actually begins and coachability kicks in at that point. You may choose to use the terms interchangeably, but this is how I see the difference between them: the timing. For reading ease though, I may use one or the other to represent them both.

Pre-screening is undertaken by the coaching custodian, sponsor or line manager and thinker before the coach gets involved, checking that **coaching is the right intervention, at the right time, for the right reasons and with the right motivation.** You'll find all the detail for this in Chapter 3.

Matching is an important aspect of coaching, and in organisations it's generally guided by the coaching custodian. If the coaching is self-funded, this is conducted purely by the thinker. You'll find all the detail for this in Chapters 4 and 5.

If they haven't done so already, the coach will then communicate with the thinker, and this is another opportunity to build coaching readiness. See Chapter 6.

This is all before the compatibility call. You might call it a chemistry call, but you can find out why we prefer compatibility in Chapter 7.

Contracting and three-way contracting (Chapters 8 and 9)

give the coach and thinker more opportunities to build coaching readiness.

Then we move to preparation for sessions, the sessions themselves and post-session integration (Chapters 10, 11 and 12), all with coaching readiness and coachability in mind.

We return to re-contracting and three-way contracting once more in Chapter 13.

And finally, we end the coaching programme in a way that enhances post-coaching agency (Chapter 14).

That's the end-to-end experience, with a reminder of the whole journey in Chapter 15.

Thereafter, I remind you about your own reflective practice as it relates to this topic of coaching readiness and coachability (Chapter 16).

And then you're done. Except you're not, as that's when your own process reviews will, I hope, take shape (if you haven't already been reviewing them as you've worked your way through the chapters). As I said before, a book is only as useful as the changes you make to your own practice. I can't make you review your processes, but I hope you'll feel encouraged and emboldened to do so with the support of your supervisor and your peers who want to change the landscape.

By the way, there may be other aspects of coaching that you'd like this book to cover. But remember that the focus is on coaching readiness and agency, not every single consideration that a coach needs to pay attention to. That would be a weighty tome! And that's what supervision is for, to ponder anything that's out of scope here. If you're new to supervision, you can find out more on the podcast I host with Steve Ridgley, *Lifting the Lid on Coaching Supervision*, available on all podcast platforms.

# Chapter 1

# Introducing coaching readiness and agency

## Why is coaching readiness important?

Coaches: wouldn't you love to be able to work at your best more of the time, with people who enable you to be your best, just as you enable them to be their best? It's time to focus on coaching readiness so that you can both bring your A-game.

> 'The most significant variable in coaching is the readiness, willingness and ability of clients to change in ways that are meaningful to them.' (Drake 2023)

If you were to transplant research from the field of psycho-therapy into your coaching world, it suggests that outcomes are predicated first and foremost not on the efficacy of the coach, but rather on the way the thinker shows up to coaching. It's not about the tools and techniques that a coach uses, but about the relation-ship that the two people build together.

As coaches, we know that there are differences between therapy and coaching, so it may be a stretch to simply transpose that research without doing any in our own field. However, some research has now been done in the coaching world about coachability. Cavanaugh et al (2021) found that growth orientation, openness, security, vulnera-bility and external resources were all important factors that coaches look for, although they do suggest that we need to do more work around how we assess for these factors so that it's not subjective.

From experience, I notice how much of a difference it makes if the thinker with whom I'm partnering plays their part in the coaching. The part they play is in:

✳ thinking for themselves
✳ making changes as a result of their new thinking.

This is at the heart of non-directive coaching, of which I am an advocate and practitioner, as I see the difference it makes when people learn for long-term sustainable growth through the hard work of thinking for themselves (Anagnostakis 2023). As she suggests:

**We must not steal the thinker's learning from them by doing it for them.**

So, if the thinker and the relationship bear the most significance on the outcomes of coaching, it's beholden on us as coaches to build that relationship and support and challenge the thinker to be coachable. They may not be intrinsically coachable, but there are ways and means by which we can cultivate it in them.

However, it's not about making the thinker wrong. Coachability 1.0 tended to be about compliance. That couldn't be further from what I'm talking about here. Coachability 2.0 is much more complex and considers a broader spectrum of stakeholders in cultivating coaching readiness. Coaching has moved on since the early days of discussion about coachability. You don't know whether someone can make the most of coaching until you start to build a relationship with them. But you can hold yourself, the thinker and all of the other stakeholders to account for getting the most out of coaching.

It would be so much more satisfying for coaches to be working with someone who really wants to be there, to do their best thinking and to make changes in their life. So, this book will help you do just that – become more fulfilled in your coaching, because you're able to screen for the coaching readiness in the thinkers with whom you work and by enhancing their coachability once coaching starts, witnessing progress in who they're becoming.

You can be more masterful in these fully collaborative partnerships compared to working with a person who has been 'voluntold' to have coaching and really doesn't want to be there with you, or when coaching isn't the right intervention for what they're facing, or when they don't know what they want to use coaching for. Wouldn't you enjoy that more, to be able to be more masterful?

⭐ I've worked with several people who want coaching but can't quite figure out how to use it for what matters most. They talk me through things they've already worked out before they come to the session, almost asking for validation of their thinking. These are all issues that they can figure out on their own, and the way they present them doesn't take the thinker further than they've already reached alone.

They aren't bringing the thorny issues for which there are no easy answers; or the issues that have been bugging them for some time that they haven't given the time to; or the things they've been avoiding because they might lead to a big change that they aren't ready for.

These people have never had coaching before and they can't quite fathom how to use it in a way that will be valuable to them. That's a problem, as they'll be disillusioned by the lack of added value they potentially walk away with. It's a problem for coaches as well, as we feel the disappointment of not being able to move them any further forward in their thinking. They've done all the thinking they're going to do.

One person in this situation told me that if he hadn't already been able to come to the answers himself, then there were no answers to be had. Yes, we're working with intelligent people who can work out things for themselves, and we want them to do that, to strengthen their thinking muscles, but why come to coaching if they're only going to tell their coach what they already know?

In these situations, it's important to re-contract around each of your roles in creating value (see Chapter 13). People sometimes realise naturally after a few sessions that there are more meaningful, important decisions that they could bring to coaching, and perhaps they were weighing up how much they could trust you and the process, but it's important that they start to create value as soon as possible. So, instigating a re-contracting conversation is key as well as continually asking them what new thinking they wish to access in the session.

In summary, coaching readiness is important for the learning it makes possible and for the fulfilment of both coach and thinker. This is the end in mind: coaching that makes an impact.

## What is coaching readiness?

'Ready clients are in motion,' writes Val Hastings (2021). 'They don't require a lot from the coach. They want to commit and take action even though they might not yet know what that looks like.'

Coachability 2.0 (a kind of overarching expression for coaching readiness and coachability, though as I've said, each is time bound) isn't about having things done to you in a passive manner! Many dictionary definitions talk about coachability as being receptive to feedback and instruction, being malleable, responsive, obliging, conformable – which is all very reactive.

These descriptions are almost the polar opposite of what I mean by coachability, which is much more proactive and comes from within the thinker: a willingness to think for themselves, having or being willing to build a sense of agency, of self-efficacy, taking the initiative, leaning in. Could there be a new dictionary definition of coachability, I wonder?!

**Your role as coach is to pull coachability out of the thinker, rather than attempting to pour something in through teaching and telling.**

How willing are they to go deep in their thinking versus superficial thinking or asking for *your* thinking? What about their willingness to make change happen in their life and work? What about their psychological readiness for that change? Homeostasis is so much more comfortable (even if it's painful) than change because it's about what we know as opposed to what we don't know (Leonard 1991). How willing are they to push past the discomfort of change?

Here's how I see coaching readiness:

Their mindset for coaching – how willing and able are they to:

* embrace their role as *thinker* in the coaching process (to think)?
* move beyond known thinking to new thinking?
* find answers that fit their unique needs, personality and context rather than a one size fits all?
* believe in their capacity to be creative, resourceful and whole?
* use their head, heart and gut to access new thinking?
* experiment in coaching and outside of it?
* focus on themselves and who they wish to be, not just the problems they need to solve?
* work on the system around them?

Their readiness for coaching – how willing and able are they to:

* introduce change into their life?
* self-select into coaching?
* move away from hooking you, their coach, into mentoring or consulting?
* identify what matters most to them to work on in coaching?
* bring their whole self to coaching – vulnerabilities, emotions and all?
* be challenged?
* work on themselves in coaching, not other people?
* look for possibilities vs impossibilities?

Thinking accelerators – how do they rate their:

* sleep quality to enable them to think clearly?
* level of physical activity to promote their mental acuity?
* frequency of being in a green space to restore their attention (whether a forest, a park, a common, a scrap of land at the end of their street)?

* diet to support critical thinking?
* intake of water to keep their brain hydrated and at peak thinking capacity?
* stress management?
* balance of their use of technology to enhance their ability to think?

Logistics – how committed are they to:

* blocking time on both sides of a coaching session, to prepare mentally and physically, and to reflect?
* turning up on time, every time?
* switching off distractions in the coaching session?
* carving out deep thinking time in their diary, over and above their coaching?

That's a lot to consider in terms of coaching readiness. This is why you need a resource such as this book to enable you to integrate these questions into your coaching screening and subsequently into cultivating more coachability along the way. See the Appendix for a questionnaire that maps to the above coaching readiness principles.

## When is coaching readiness important?

I've hinted at the idea that coaching readiness and coachability aren't a once-and-done aspect of screening and the chemistry session. In this book, I'll look at the end-to-end coaching experience, including pre-screening, screening, contracting and re-contracting, session-by-session coaching readiness and coachability, and closing for agency.

Coaching readiness, coachability and agency are always important and they can wax and wane, so you need to bring it into your own and the thinker's awareness and discuss how to nurture it at any given time in the coaching process.

As I said previously, I'm coming to realise that you might use the expression coaching readiness before coaching starts – are they ready for this? – and coachability or agency during coaching. See what you think as you read on. Maybe there's an umbrella word or phrase that spans the whole coaching experience. I haven't figured that out yet – I wonder whether it might come to you as you consider this subject.

There's a belief in some parts of the coaching profession that we can coach anyone in any context. Yes, we can trust that the process of coaching will work with most people in most contexts, but my experience of coaching in the National Health Service, for example, is very different from working with people in the corporate world due to the water within which they swim rather than the individuals themselves. This means that no matter how coachable the individual might be, they may feel stymied by the seeming impossibilities created by the system around them. These impossibilities are often complex, involving multiple competing or unhelpful processes, people, resources and technology. Every system creates its own limitations for the people who work within it. So, while coaching readiness is important in every context, don't forget that you're working with human beings who are fallible and in some cases work under some extremely difficult conditions that make their readiness for coaching incredibly hard. That's not to make them victims of circumstance, but to recognise that seeing the glimmers of hope may be tougher in some situations.

Your role as a coach is to support them in these difficult, sometimes frustrating circumstances as well as to enable them to look for even the smallest of opportunities that are within their control.

## What prevents you from screening for coaching readiness at the start of a coaching process?

So, you know why coaching readiness is important to you as the coach and to the thinkers with whom you work. But frequently, you'll make a mistake and start working with someone even when your intuition was quietly (or loudly) telling you that the thinker might not be ready for coaching: maybe it isn't the right time, coaching isn't the best-fit intervention for their needs or maybe they just plain don't want it.

Proceeding despite signals that perhaps you shouldn't may be driven by financial insecurity: independent coaches need money to live. Whether you're an internal or external coach, proceeding may be driven by a desire to accumulate hours towards a credential so that you can get there sooner. It may be that you just don't feel equipped to say no. Or, as a newbie, you may think that if you only tried harder, you could crack this nut. Maybe, maybe not! It depends what you mean by trying harder.

Maybe you've never come across this idea of screening or all of its constituent parts. Don't feel bad about that if your training didn't cover it. I've said previously that most training teaches you to coach and that in itself is a set of skills that needs constant refining. But this piece is just as important so that you don't start to doubt your coaching skills when it may actually be the thinker who's not playing their part.

I don't mean to sound as if I lack compassion for the people you might work with, but I do want to be blunt here to give you permission, if you need it, to turn down gigs that won't be fulfilling. Please understand that not all money is worth the hassle and not all hours of coaching are worth the frustration.

**It's good to gain experience, but not if it messes with your head and your belief in yourself as a coach.**

Contrary to what your coach training might have taught you, you can't coach everyone! There are some red flags that your intuition will recognise and which you need your brain to pay attention to. And even if you didn't listen to your intuition at the start, you can always re-contract when it becomes obvious that the thinker isn't playing their part and is overstepping boundaries. Or you can end the contract gracefully and with compassion – more of which in due course.

## Summary

Paying attention to coaching readiness before coaching and coachability during coaching is vital for the success of coaching – success meaning the amount of value that a thinker can extract for themselves, building their own thinking muscles, understanding themselves and being able to articulate their needs.

**It's in your gift to screen for coaching readiness and draw out coachability in partnership with each thinker with whom you work – and their stakeholders – and it will be different for each person, depending on their starting point.**

### Reflective practice

❊ What do *you* believe about what you've read so far?

❊ Which of your values are showing up (or even being triggered) as you read this chapter? What does that tell you?

❊ What will you ask for and from whom? Which of these boundaries are non-negotiable and in which circumstances might you flex?

❊ What's the one thing you'll commit to experiment with that will make a marginal gain in the coaching readiness of the people with whom you work?

# Chapter 2

# The signs and signals of coaching readiness

## Relationships are complex

Before I dig into the signs and signals of coaching readiness, one caveat: all relationships are complex. We build each relationship one interaction at a time, so there are very few reasons to discount working with someone from the outset on the basis of a lack of coaching readiness.

The way people present themselves is also complex. The prospective thinker may be feeling – and acting – defeated as they come into coaching. **Part of your work together might be to get them back into a creative state, whereby they can see the glimmers of hope.**

Their defeatism may not be because of who they are but rather they might have lost their self-agency due to impossible systemic issues in their organisation – an interwoven combination of lack of people, lack of funds, lack of joined-up thinking, huge pressures from outside the organisation, highly challenging situations with low support systems in place, and more. This isn't a situation that the thinker (alone) created! In these circumstances, you can enable them to find those glimmers of hope rather than falling into the trap of victimhood and stuckness. Please don't claim that you can co-create some magical 'big bang' overhaul. This isn't about unbridled optimism. Optimism (according to Roman Krznaric 2021) can breed complacency and inaction, where hope recognises the real possibility of failure while at the same time holding on to the prospect of success despite the odds. **And coaching isn't all about the big bang; sometimes it's more of a slow burn.**

People are predisposed to look for their own and systemic

limitations. This is a very human trait (Hanson 2013). But at the other end of the spectrum from defeatism, people may be looking at everything through rose-tinted glasses, perhaps lacking in self-awareness, blind to the reality of the situation, overly optimistic. Your antennae need to be picking up the data about strengths and overused strengths that a person presents with, not just the limitations. No matter how people arrive in this space, defeatist or overoptimistic, they still need to be coaching ready.

# Signs and signals to pay attention to

All that being said, when you're in conversation with an individual, there are certain things you can look out for in the individual themselves, whether they're paying for the coaching privately or being funded by their organisation.

## Is coaching the best-fit intervention to meet the individual's hopes and intentions?

**We assume that prospective thinkers are robust enough for the process – until they're not.**

They must think they are, otherwise they wouldn't be exploring coaching. However, they may not know the difference between the available interventions or even what the available interventions might be. That becomes part of the initiation into coaching, helping them to understand what they'll get from this process compared to any other, thus enabling them to make a conscious choice about whether to proceed. They're not necessarily experienced buyers of coaching and don't know what they don't know. But, as I've said, treat the thinker as 'creative, resourceful and whole' and believe that they can figure out their needs when they have enough time to slow down and think about them, with some questions to support their exploration of options.

In your initial conversation with them, they might share with you that they've had therapy in the past or are in therapy now. This opens the door for you to have a candid conversation about what they hope coaching might offer them that they're not getting in therapy, and whether their therapist is happy for you to proceed concurrently with that therapy. But they might not be so overt. They might hint at some issues that might possibly be more pertinent to a therapeutic intervention, such as a father who didn't believe in them or grief from a recent or not so recent loss. These subtle remarks give you licence to enquire further and decide together whether coaching is sufficient to support them. You mustn't shy away from checking these out, though it's not in your remit to diagnose. There's nothing to be gained by glossing over these seemingly throwaway admissions, though you can explain the difference with real examples of how coaching and therapy differ, for example:

✳ In therapy, you'd likely talk about how to fix the relationship with the thinker's father or how to decrease feelings related to their relationship with their father.
✳ In coaching, you wouldn't work on the relationship with the father, but rather how the relationship is having an impact on current relationships and how the thinker might work on themselves to rectify those present-day relationships. This is all about how to have better conversations.
✳ If appropriate, therapy can be simultaneous – it doesn't automatically have to be an either/or. For more insights into this, you may wish to read the paper in the bibliography from the ICF about when and how to refer a person (Hullinger & DiGirolamo 2018). One caveat: please check out the implications around referral for your country and insurance coverage. In the UK, for example, you can provide a listing but cannot signpost to a particular individual, as that would be construed as advice.

Sometimes, the thinker may hold back until they feel safe with you, meaning that they don't divulge any of these things until you've been working together for a while. Again, once they share it, this enables you to have a conversation about what they deem to be best for them.

Coaches can still lean into emotion caused in the present, so work with their humanity rather than shying away from it. You *are* equipped to work with current emotion, but not so much with trauma experienced in the past (see Shift 36 in *The Transformational Coach*).

Coaching also relies on hope, so if a person is feeling or showing signs of helplessness and hopelessness, you might ask them what impact it's having on them and how it might impact on the coaching, then ask them how they'd like to resource themselves – not necessarily instead of coaching, but at least in conjunction with it. You're not making any diagnoses here, but merely providing information about professionals who have the expertise to do so. That said, if they're in immediate danger to themselves or to others, it's your duty of care as a human being to stay with them (virtually or in person) and phone the emergency services (for more insights, see Michael Marx's 2018 article).

What's the organisational contract with regard to the scope of the coaching? What's in scope and what's out of scope in coaching conversations? How would the organisation feel if a coach were straying into therapeutic territory, even if the coach was trained to move into that space (for example)?

The coaching and/or therapy choice is just one of many. There's also the coaching and/or medical choice. For example, what if they relay that they're drinking to excess? In this case you might ask them how that might impact on the coaching and where else they might go for support with that.

Your role is to look at resourcing them, not advising them where to go, but you can share information with them such as a link to the Hub of Hope or Mind (both UK based), which will provide them with validated options that are in their location.

However, this is complex territory. If your paying client is an organisation, the contract might stipulate what you have to do. For example, law firms are regulated by their governing body, which sets out what's meant to happen if someone is breaching the code of conduct/ethics, including drink/drugs, etc. Be sure not to put yourself into a breach of contract situation.

What if the thinker declares that they have brain fog and are struggling to think straight? Coaching relies on clear thinking (and feeling and sensing), so again you might ask them what they think it's about, what the impact on coaching might be and where they might go for support with that. You aren't diagnosing; you're resourcing and providing information that they can choose – or not – to research.

If they ask for more of a mentoring approach or consultancy, the thinker's hopes and intentions for coaching may convey a misunderstanding of coaching. You need to test this out with them, enabling them to decide whether they really want mentoring or coaching. If it's the former, you can triage that and help them to choose someone they might ask to mentor them. If it's the latter, it's important that they understand before they sign up for the coaching what that really means in terms of the expectations for them to do the hard work of thinking.

Please bear in mind that any liability insurance you've taken out for your coaching practice may not cover you for giving advice of any kind – for example, about what kind of practitioner to consult. Human beings are complex, and you may not know the full history. You can encourage, you can give information, but you shouldn't be advising them who to see. However, you should tell them when you're not the right practitioner and in that instance you can support them to resource themselves differently. It's not your responsibility to make them seek that support, except in a crisis. If in doubt, speak to your supervisor about whether you're genuinely the best person to support them at this moment in time.

My thanks to Anne Archer, a Mental Health First Aid trainer for coaches, for her guidance here.

## Is coaching the best-fit intervention to meet the organisation's hopes and intentions?

Line managers sometimes neglect to give constructive, stretch feedback until it's too late and the individual has derailed. They might then make a request of the coaching custodian for coaching for the individual. If this is billed as 'the last chance' for the individual, you should be asking questions about what has gone before. Did the line manager play their managerial part or did they shirk the responsibility of giving feedback? The latter isn't a satisfactory set-up from which to start coaching and a coach might be better placed to decline this invitation, at least until that feedback has been given and the line manager has accepted responsibility for the part they played in this. It's not the coach's role to become the messenger. What's the organisation doing to prevent this in the first place? What expectations are placed on line managers as part of their objectives to manage people, not just projects? What support are they giving to line managers to give feedback early and often?

Line managers not giving feedback is a common issue. And there are others: the thinker may need training – for example, if this is their first managerial role. Coaching can't fill the gaps in their knowledge about how to manage people. It could work alongside this training or after it to embed the learning in their own day-to-day realities, but coaching isn't a substitute for training.

⭐ One of my most frustrating coaching partnerships was with someone who, it turned out, had never been offered any training for his new role as a manager of people. He did want coaching, but despite my explanation about him doing the thinking for himself, he didn't really know what it meant and kept trying to hook me into telling him what to do.

According to the Peter Principle (Peter & Hull 1969), high-performing individual contributors are often promoted beyond their level of competence. Managing and leading others is a totally different skill to the technical proficiency they've demonstrated in the past. But if organisations were to put training in place to plug that gap, this lack of knowledge and application about leading others need not be perpetuated. The coaching could then be a support mechanism to help the individual translate the theory for their unique team members. Non-directive coaching wasn't what he needed at this point – training was.

You might say, well, just come out of non-directive coaching and be more of a mentor. I used to teach leadership skills, so in theory I could do that. But this wasn't what I was commissioned for and I'm not necessarily the best person for that teaching role any more as I don't keep up with the latest research in that field. I'd also prefer to spend my time working on who the person wishes to be as a leader, not what they do – that's where I get the most satisfaction and it's a choice about the kind of work I want to be doing. And, last but not least, I believe so strongly in the power of non-directive coaching, used at the right time (in this case, after training) to build a person's belief in themselves. All of the research into self-directed thinking leads me to take this stand. But at the time, I didn't take a stand, to both of our detriments. I've learned from this experience to screen much more thoroughly around whether coaching is the best fit at this point in time.

Coaching is also not a substitute for a developmental opportunity to learn on the job – a stretch assignment, if you like, that enables the thinker to learn on the job with support from their manager.

Maybe some other organisational intervention might be more appropriate when they're overwhelmed with the magnitude of the workload, for example reallocating some of the work to others, restructuring the team or taking them off a particular client/project. **Coaching is not the panacea for inattentive management practice.**

It might help the thinker to ask for what they need from their manager, but coaching must never be seen as a substitute for good quality management.

See Chapter 9 on tripartite contracting for more in-depth

suggestions around mining for the hopes and intentions of the organisation.

## Does the individual want coaching?

Individuals who are self-funding generally want coaching; they wouldn't be researching it if they didn't (although, at the early stage of their investigations, they may not know whether coaching is the intervention that will meet their needs). Sometimes, though, you may encounter someone who's self-funding and yet suggests in a resigned way that they've worked with other coaches before and nothing has changed for them – putting huge pressure on you to wave a magic wand. They want coaching and yet they may not want to do the hard work; what they perhaps expect is for you to find the breakthrough, rather than finding it for themselves. You'll need to contract around how they can resource themselves in this process rather than being rescued, both within the coaching sessions and in between, and whether they're willing to invest in themselves in this way, voicing their own needs and making things happen. Returning to the personal trainer analogy from earlier in the book, a person might have a personal training session once or twice a week, but unless they're willing to train in between, they won't become as fit and strong as they might like to be. The same is true of coaching: unless the thinker is willing to put in the work in between sessions, no coach will be able to provide them with the changes that they're hoping for.

Those whose organisations are paying for the coaching may have been put forward for coaching and may not be keen. If they feel that the organisation is willing to invest this money in them, they may feel that the organisation must value them, so they're willing to give it a try. At other times, they may feel forced into it and go along with it despite their misgivings.

Decide together whether coaching is not for them, and also decide together how to explain that to the coaching custodian or line manager who has put them forward for coaching. Help them explore how else they might meet their need so that they can ask for that: for example, training, a development opportunity, work taken off their plate, etc.

> ⭐ I once met a potential thinker who'd had what she described as mediocre coaching in the past, so she wasn't sure whether this was for her, despite her line manager's encouragement. She met a couple of coaches before deciding she'd like to proceed on her own terms. The thinker will be considering levels of trust, feelings of agency and belief in confidentiality. Together, you must also consider levels of agency. Check out what part the thinker played in the coaching turning out to be mediocre. It may not have been all about the coaches with whom they worked.

If the potential thinker is giving off what you perceive to be signals that they don't want the coaching, it may be because they're not invested in their role or the organisation. It's nothing personal towards the coach, though it might feel that way. **Ask them about the data you see in their body language and tone of voice; don't presume to know what it means.**

Have a 'normal' conversation rather than a coaching conversation, to start to build trust but also to get insights into what's working and what's not, without manipulating them to divulge when they're not comfortable to do so. This might lead them to understand any organisational hurt that coaching could support them to work through.

Organisations sometimes use coaching before, during or after leadership training. In this instance, the participants in the training may not particularly want coaching nor know how to use it. It just comes as part of the package. They may be expecting more of the same: teaching, mentoring, training. Some of the candidates will embrace their different role in coaching; others may not. It's important that the coach and prospective thinker decide together whether or not coaching will be valuable to them at this stage in their career. They may just give it a go to start with, but find that it isn't giving them what they want because they were unclear on what they wanted. It's OK to call it a day after a few sessions. There's no judgement, but again it's important to be congruent in how you report back to the coaching custodian or sponsor.

## Does the individual think they need coaching?

Some people think they're already the bee's knees, with perhaps an unreasonable sense of their own importance. Hogan (2017) describes this as 'fantasised talent': people who believe they're 'born for greatness, inventive, arrogant, hyper-competitive, unrealistic'. It's not so much that they don't *want* coaching as believing that they don't *need* coaching. It's difficult (though not impossible) to work with someone who's unwilling to be vulnerable and admit to things that aren't working. It's their prerogative to turn down the coaching and it's best to call a halt to it at the start. If you were to move forward, the thinker might bring issues that have little meaning for them or are insignificant in nature. It would be frustrating for both parties to 'waste' time on something that's not deemed to be a necessity. Bear in mind that at the early stages of coaching, psychological safety hasn't yet been built, so there are limits to how vulnerable a person may be willing to be. But I repeat, ask them whether they believe they need coaching and for what purpose, and if they do, contract for the way you'll work together.

In another scenario, maybe the thinker has tried everything (to their mind) already, nothing has worked and nothing else is possible. The tone of voice that goes with this can give us different signals. Is the tone arrogant (this is your judgement, of course, rather than fact), suggesting that coaching will never be clever enough to enable them to find a breakthrough? Or is the tone more defeatist due to the organisational limitations and restrictions? If it's the latter, you may still be able to work together to find the glimmers of hope. However, a reminder once again not to interpret the tone of voice yourself, but rather to ask what it means. It's data, not fact – and none of this is binary.

**There are never clear lines of distinction, such as, 'If this happens, then do that'.** Take it to supervision to process the particulars of your situation.

Some potential thinkers might believe that all of their woes are caused by other people; they lay the blame onto others. They're not self-aware or willing enough to recognise the part that they play in the dysfunction of the relationship. Coaching can't work for people who aren't in the room, and the person who is in the room needs to be willing to work on themselves as a constituent part of the relationship difficulties.

The organisation may decide to send a perceived narcissist to coaching because they're harming the people around them and showing little care for them. Coach, beware! Check this out in conversation with the coaching custodian or sponsor before agreeing to a chemistry session. Think carefully before agreeing to partner with this kind of thinker – it's unlikely to be a partnership as they won't put in the requisite work and may even try to harm you through their words and actions.

## Is the individual willing to put in the work of thinking and changing?

Does the potential thinker have an end in mind for the coaching? It's a great start if they know what they want to be different by the time the coaching is complete. They may not know exactly what they want that future to look, feel or sound like, but perhaps they know that things can't go on the way they are. Either way, they're eager for change of some sort. You can work together to establish exactly what that change might be.

Putting in the work to get there is a coachable trait. It's not enough to hope for the best, but rather to be prepared to spend time in between coaching sessions making small tweaks and course corrections to the way they live and work.

**Coaching isn't magic, and change won't happen without deep thinking, commitment and willingness to change.** It's important that the thinker knows this right from the start. The hard work of thinking and acting will be done by them, not by the coach. They, not the coach, will hold themselves accountable for the promises they make to themselves about progress. They are adults and you must invite them into that space, rather than you adopting a teacher-like (parental) approach to accountability that disempowers their adulthood and pushes them into child-like compliance (see Berne 1964 and Chapter 11).

# Summary

In summary, these are questions to be paying attention to as you begin a coaching assignment:

* Is coaching the best-fit intervention to meet the individual's and the organisation's hopes and intentions?
* Does the individual want coaching?
* Do they need coaching?
* Are they willing to put in the work of thinking and of changing, of stepping into 'Adult'?

Bear in mind that everything is data.

**Hone your ability to pick up on the data and ask the thinker to analyse that data rather than doing so yourself.**

Ask them what their body language, tone of voice, timeliness or contribution means rather than making a judgement that might be wide of the mark.

## Reflective practice

* What do *you* believe about the signs and signals of coaching readiness?
* Which of your values are showing up (or even being triggered) as you read this chapter? What does that tell you?
* What will you ask for and from whom? Which of these boundaries are non-negotiable and in which circumstances might you flex?
* What's the one thing you'll commit to experiment with that will make a marginal gain in the coaching readiness of the people with whom you work?

# Chapter 3

# Pre-screening through a coaching readiness lens

*Written in collaboration with Sam Humphrey*

When working within an organisational setting (or through an associate company or coaching platform), internal and external coaches will need to work with and through the person or people who are responsible for coaching in that organisation – the coaching custodians.

This coaching custodian has the authority and capability to shape the coaching infrastructure in their organisation, including the strategic set-up, the operational plan and the tactical processes of coaching. They need not hold the budget for coaching nor have the final say on how it's spent; however, they may have significant influence over the criteria upon which spending decisions are taken.

Coaching custodians are typically HR (human resources), L&D (learning and development) or talent professionals who understand the need for people processes to have purpose, definition, scope, roles and responsibilities and more crucially business value.

Why include the coaching custodian in a book about coaching readiness/coachability? Because coaching readiness is greatly informed by the way in which coaching is introduced to a potential thinker in an organisation and that is facilitated by the coaching custodian.

**Our intention for this chapter is to enable you to urge and mobilise coaching custodians to scrutinise their screening processes to safeguard coaching programmes and position them to realise value for all parties.**

In the interests of simplicity, we'll focus here on the custodian within an organisation, but please also consider this for your work through associate companies and coaching platforms. At the end of the chapter, we reflect upon how you might decide to take a stand for better screening if it's absent.

What we describe here is a robust process. We fully understand that organisations make decisions about where to place their budgets and that some coaching custodians' time is therefore stretched thin. There are consequences to this for the return on expectations of coaching programmes. We argue that decisions must be made strategically, knowing the full repercussions of those actions. We hope to be able to articulate why investment in the role of the coaching custodian is vital to the success of coaching – and, in this case, to the coaching readiness of the thinker.

⭐ Why would you, a coach, want to have an influence over the coaching custodian's processes? We've been hearing in supervision and other coaching circles how some coaches are feeling impoverished by the low quality of screening that's taking place.

Coaches who are signed up with coaching platforms in particular are finding it to be a bit of a slog (their word). They start it to gain hours and experience and a regular income, but often find that thinkers haven't been well briefed and try to hook the coach into mentoring; and the coach is doing a lot of the heavy lifting rather than it being a partnership.

They feel a lack of agency in who they're matched with – and no sense that they can say no when there isn't a good match, for example; and they sometimes have to work to a formula dictated by the platform. Some platforms also measure coaching with assessment questions that miss out on agency and learning as outcomes in their own right.

Coaches feel like a supplier rather than a partner, influencer or consultant to the platform. I'm not saying that all coaching platforms are created equal, and there are some positive reviews too, but some coaches have lost the joy of coaching as a result of working with coaching platforms to get their work. This is all to do with the inadequate set-up of the coaching before the coach gets involved. This is one reason why you should read these chapters, so that you feel empowered to speak up for what could be different, and so that you can reclaim the joy.

Coaching has been an established leadership development intervention for years now and the infrastructure of coaching has also been the subject of change, driven by internal and external factors. As a result, many organisations have a coaching infrastructure that's a bit of a Frankenstein's monster, where different aspects of coaching have been introduced or tweaked at different times by different coaching custodians.

Where this is the case, we'd recommend that coaches encourage the coaching custodian to undertake Grit's coaching infrastructure audit to ensure it's fit for purpose. The output of this process is a comprehensive risk profile report, created in discussion with clients, which categorises those areas that are fit for purpose and those that fall short.

For the purposes of this chapter, we'll assume that the coaching custodian has already gone through this process and has clarity on aspects including:

* the business rationale for coaching in this organisation
* the purpose of coaching to meet the needs of the organisation
* the relevant stakeholders and sponsors of a coaching programme
* the coaching pool – selection criteria and assessment/ selection process
* where coaching is useful and where it is not
* what kind of coaching programmes will be put in place, that is, programme led, individual development led, business driven, goal led, etc

* measures of success for coaching programmes, tied to the business strategy
* whether and how to use internal and/or external coaches
* how to harvest the learning at a systemic level
* the technology to support a coaching programme.

The above points are outside the scope of this book, which focuses on the coaching readiness of the *thinker*, but they do have a significant impact on the coaching readiness of the *organisation*. You can find out more about these prerequisites by visiting grit. co.uk for a coaching infrastructure audit.

Chapter 5 will cover the set-up for private coaching contracts, commissioned directly by a potential thinker, but don't skip these chapters about organisational screening as there will be ideas that you can use with self-funded coaching partnerships too. This chapter will focus on organisational coaching and cover the following:

* the business case for screening, for all parties
* the purpose of screening, for all parties
* good practice for screening, depending on the type of coaching
* tips for coaches, both internal and external, where the above is not in place.

## The business case for pre-screening

You might be asking what the driving force is for coaching custodians to spend time screening for coaching readiness. They're busy people, so adding this onto their plate (if it's not already on it) might feel like the proverbial straw that broke the camel's back. But there are many reasons for investing time here to ensure that the coaching pays dividends in the long run.

We'll first look at the risks of not screening, then the compelling case for change for each of the parties involved, culminating in the outcomes an organisation can expect from enhancing their screening process before a coach even gets involved. The precise economic analysis is beyond the scope of this book but, as with so many areas in life, the more effort that's put in upfront, the more time and money will be saved later.

**What are the risks of not screening for coaching readiness? The organisation won't get the return on investment/expectations that they hope for.**

This is due in part to the following reasons:

* Coaching may not be the best intervention for the thinker and/or for the issues that they're facing.
* Coaching may be used to 'outsource' problem employees to a coach, thus removing people management responsibilities from the line manager and undermining their development as a leader.
* If it's seen not to be working due to an incomplete screening process, coaching may be questioned by the organisational budget-holders. This causes stress in the system and particularly for the coaching custodian.
* The thinker may come to coaching confused about what it is and is not. Confusion leads to stress, which in turn leads to difficulty in thinking straight (Craig 2012).
* The thinker won't be prepared for the amount of hard thinking that's involved in coaching, and may become frustrated that they're not getting what they thought they were signing up for.
* The coach may become frustrated as the thinker attempts to hook them into mentoring or consulting, or doesn't dedicate time or effort at all.
* There may be missed opportunities for more applicable interventions such as training or on-the-job stretch assignments with feedback (to name just a couple).

We've alluded above to the various parties who have a stake in the success or otherwise of the coaching. Making those more explicit, we'll look at:

1. the organisation
2. the coaching custodian
3. the coach
4. the thinker
5. the line manager or sponsor of the thinker.

Taking each in turn, let's dive a little deeper.

1. **The organisation:** The price tag of coaching requires it to be successful (however that's defined in that organisation's culture). It's out of the scope of this book to delve into return on investment, but that's what the organisation needs from this expense on the balance sheet. One element that will lead to a more successful coaching arrangement is the efficacy (or otherwise) of the screening process, ensuring that each party knows their role in the process and supports the thinker to make the changes.

2. **The coaching custodian:** This person may want to prove their worth as they shepherd a coaching programme that brings business results. They'll be providing visibility to the ethics and integrity of the coaching programme. They can also save themself hassle in the latter stages of a coaching programme by getting it right first time – screening for coaching readiness, as far as that's possible.

3. **The coach:** Whether internal or external, the coach will be able to spend more quality time coaching the thinker if the screening has been done before they start their work with the thinker. You'll be grateful to the coaching custodian for smoothing the way, so that the thinker turns up to a chemistry session or first coaching session motivated and ready to do the hard work of thinking, understanding what coaching is and is not, knowing that this is the intervention that best fits their needs and having a sense of the partnership that will be created. This is so much more fulfilling for you than having to cover the basics before digging into the relationship building and the work itself.

4. **The thinker:** As noted above, the thinker will know what this thing called coaching is all about. They'll know what their role is in the partnership. Sure, they might have heard the explanation without it really sinking in, but at least they'll have heard it once before coming to the coach, and they'll know that this is a good fit for their needs. Hope will be building in them before they even come to the coaching (Green et al 2007). They'll likely already be thinking through their challenges and perhaps even resolving some of them pre-coaching, thus taking the quick wins off the table. As a result, they'll start to realise that putting their focus onto what matters most gives it the attention it deserves and allows for sorting and sifting through issues and opportunities – as the science would have it, neuroplasticity (Rock & Schwartz 2006).

5. **The line manager/sponsor of the thinker:** Chances are, the line manager will gain from a successful coaching programme, as the thinker becomes more aligned with what they want from their work and life. That might be in the form of the thinker taking more of the load off the shoulders of the line manager. Or it might be that the thinker decides that this isn't the place for them to be their authentic self, which is also a win in the long run, as the manager can find someone for this role who cares about the work and has strengths that are a better fit for the job. Sometimes the thinker wants to use coaching to improve their relationship with their line manager, another gain for both parties. We include sponsors in the mix here, as CEOs rarely have a line manager but will have a board director to whom they're accountable.

All the above depends on a good screening process in the first place to ensure that:

※ coaching is a good fit for the intentions of the thinker and the organisation

※ the thinker shows up with a clear view of what they'd like to use coaching for, ready to think for themselves and willing to change in some way

✳ the coach can do the job they're paid to do – which is coaching

✳ all other parties understand their role in the success of the coaching rather than expecting the coaching custodian and/ or the coach to take the lead.

# The purpose of pre-screening

We propose that there are three stakeholders that benefit from screening for a coaching assignment, namely the coach, the thinker and the organisation. Coach screening isn't covered in this book, and you can find more on this topic in the Grit Coaching Value Chain (grit.co.uk).

McKenna and Davis (2009) conducted research into what makes for a successful therapeutic intervention. They highlighted four key components which, although not focused on coaching, are interesting to consider in the context of the coaching world.

**The first component for success relates to the thinker and external factors, and the second to the relationship between the coach and the thinker.**

In the original research, the former accounted for 40 per cent of the success of an intervention and the latter 30 per cent.

Assuming these factors have significant resonance in coaching, it suggests you should attach importance to the set-up for both the thinker and for you as coach.

Before any screening starts, the coaching custodian and/or the thinker need to give thought to what they're expecting of the coaching. One approach is to explore the type of coaching that's required. Examples in the business context may include the following.

1. **Business-driven coaching:** This type of coaching programme is often designed for senior leaders in a business with systemic reach and influence. The value lies in ensuring the

work attends to the needs of the individual *and* the system. This coaching tends to be holistic and focuses less on goals, as the coaching outcomes are more emergent in nature. As coaches, we know this type of coaching work can demand a lot from the thinker as the organisational needs aren't necessarily the same as the individual's wants!

2. **Individual development needs coaching:** This type of coaching programme is typically designed for people the organisation wants to transition from good to great. The value lies in increasing self-awareness, broadening perspectives, accelerating the ramp-up time to proficiency in a new role and maximising opportunities (playing to win, not playing to avoid losing). This work is often based around what the individual needs and wants from being coached and usually has a strong focus on goals.

3. **Goal-led coaching:** This type of coaching is intended to deliver a specific outcome, skill or behaviour. The value tends to focus on the outcome rather than the process within it.

4. **Programme-led coaching**: This type of coaching is normally attached to a course or development programme. The point at which the coaching is deployed determines where the value could be – for example, if the coaching precedes the programme, the value could be in preparing the thinker to glean maximum value from the programme. If the coaching runs during the programme, the value could be the immediate transfer of the programme content and learning into everyday work. And if the coaching runs after the programme, the value could be in reflecting on how the content and learning could most usefully impact the longer term or strategic needs of the business or individual.

Clarity on the type of coaching the coaching custodian wants to deploy in the organisation enables them to create coach and thinker screening criteria.

We recognise that these are organisation specific, and this

doesn't minimise the importance of coaching outside organisations, which may include personally funded career coaching, retirement coaching, vision coaching or any number of other types of self-funded coaching. We address the process for this in Chapter 5.

We think it's important to distinguish screening criteria from matching criteria as they serve very different purposes. Screening criteria are intended to:

✳ enable the coaching custodian to determine the assessment and selection process they wish to put in place to ensure they have coaches that can deliver the type of coaching required
✳ ensure they have thinkers who are ready, willing and able to derive value from coaching.

Matching criteria, on the other hand, serve to inform how to secure the best coach/thinker combination to deliver the anticipated outcome. This is covered in more detail in Chapter 4.

The remainder of this chapter will focus on what's involved in screening the thinker to ensure they're compatible with coaching.

## Thinker screening

In most organisations, there are HR or L&D specialists who are skilled at needs analysis. This is useful in determining if coaching is the 'right' intervention but is different from assessing whether the thinker is 'right' for coaching. Many organisations also have a gatekeeper role in coaching, but this typically relates to approval of budget rather than approving coaching as the best fit for the thinker.

Typically, the coaching custodian receives a request for coaching along the following lines, and these requests will often require screening:

✳ a direct request from the thinker
✳ a line manager request
✳ an HR/L&D suggestion

* a post annual appraisal option
* an offer attached to a promotion or new joiner or transitioner (such as maternity/paternity leave, retirement)
* an automatic requirement attached to a programme or initiative.

Internal coaches sometimes get direct referrals from past thinkers or line managers who know that they coach. In this instance, the internal coach should involve the coaching custodian to screen and match. This will ensure that the potential thinker is coaching ready and that they're matched with a coach who's the best fit for them, rather than the only one known to the referrer.

Wherever internal referrals and requests emanate from, it's worth making sure that there's a consistency of understanding about what makes for coaching readiness. Line managers, for example, don't always understand that the thinker must be willing to enter into a coaching relationship; it can't be forced on them. Line managers often think coaching is about fixing people rather than taking them from good to great. I've (Clare) heard of an example where a person's line manager put them forward for coaching because of a perceived wrongdoing, where the individual didn't accept that they were doing anything untoward at all. This is not a good case for coaching.

Thinker-screening criteria are perhaps not as straightforward as coach-screening criteria as there isn't a set of recognised 'thinker competencies'. That said, there are several researched factors that predict a positive shift in performance and the most common (based on Asay & Lambert 1999) include:

* level of motivation to engage in the coaching and to reach a positive outcome
* ability to cope/style of coping
* intelligence
* openness to feedback and/or to the experience
* learning orientation
* level of self-awareness

* level of self-efficacy
* ownership and acceptance of the proposed need to change
* commitment to making change happen
* importance of the issue/opportunity
* urgency.

Another way to think about screening a thinker's readiness for change is to apply the work of Prochaska et al. The book *Changing for Good* (1994) describes six stages of change that an individual goes through in order to change a habit or way of behaving:

1. precontemplation
2. contemplation
3. preparation
4. action
5. maintenance
6. termination.

Prochaska et al note that: **behaviour change rarely happens as a result of an imposition by others; rather it requires an individual to change themselves to a new way of behaving.**

Each stage of this change model holds different challenges, and understanding what stage the thinker is at will identify their state of readiness for change.

Recognising which stage applies to the thinker will give you a sense of their readiness to be coached and enable you to jointly make choices about what changes they'll make and how they'll make them. It also enables you and the thinker, together, to see shifts throughout as the coaching work progresses and the thinker moves through these stages. In an ideal world, you'd work alongside thinkers until they reach the penultimate stage of maintenance, thus enabling you both to determine and put in place strategies to avoid relapses to old mindsets and behaviour and/or tactics to move on from a relapse (termination, where people have no desire to return to their old ways of being, being the final and rare stage of change).

Our hope is that the coaching custodian might use a version

of the table below to inform a conversation with a potential thinker about their self-perceived readiness for change. This can be shared with the coach as part of the coaching brief (see page 60). If this isn't possible, the coach may wish to use this with the thinker directly either as a one-pager for self-assessment or as part of the chemistry session.

# ↻ Readiness for change

| Stage | What you might hear | What you might see |
|---|---|---|
| Pre-con-templation | 'I don't think I have a problem' | • Repeating the same behaviours<br>• Denial about the problems that the behaviour is creating<br>• Talking as though they're a victim of circumstances<br>• No desire or intention to change |
| Contempla-tion | 'I want to stop feeling so stuck' | • Stuckness, not sure how best to proceed<br>• Say they want to change but not doing anything about it or not sure what to do about it, other than talking about it<br>• Might have conceptual plans without concrete ways forward |
| Preparation | 'I'm going to change' | • Public declarations of change<br>• Getting themselves ready to make change happen, with some hesitation<br>• Still some unresolved ambivalence |
| Action | 'I'm very confident I can make this happen' | • Confidence that could tip into overconfidence<br>• Lots of visible action and changes related to the goal<br>• Progress, achievement<br>• Also, internal shifts in mood, self-belief, ways of seeing the world |
| Mainte-nance | 'I failed' | • Reverting to old behaviour<br>• Frustration that the change hasn't happened or they're stuck<br>• Floundering |

In addition to the above factors, the coaching custodian should think about other factors that could impact the performance of the thinker, for example:

* What has been done already to effect the required change?
* What's the thinker's tenure in the role (transitioning into a new role or well established)?
* Are there any health or personal circumstances that might impact the coaching?
* Have they been coached before and how successful was that?

# Organisational pre-screening

The final screening that's wise to consider is that of the organisation itself. To ensure that coaching fits with the culture and norms of the organisation, it can be useful to consider the following questions:

* Is this the best timing for the coaching, based on the annual rhythm of the organisation/role?
* Are there any upcoming changes in the organisational structure that might impact the coaching or the timing of it?
* What other demands might the thinker be drawn into that would detract from or alter the coaching?
* Does the organisation's culture support coaching as an intervention?
* Is the thinker's leadership supportive of coaching and will they be prepared to make changes to enable the coaching to be successful?

**Encouraging the coaching custodian to establish a checklist of criteria they think are important for the coaching to be impactful will ensure the set-up is both thorough and well considered.**

Explicitly screening and assessing the thinker and the coach and also considering the organisational context for the coaching significantly impacts the chances of the coaching being successful.

## Thinker assessment processes

Thinkers' requests for coaching are typically assessed through:

✳ self-assessment by the thinker against a list of criteria and a justification for coaching, including the business and/or individual benefit
✳ line management and/or HR/L&D approval against a list of criteria and a business/individual need identified, agreed and sanctioned to go ahead.

Good practice would be to encourage organisations to create a thinker assessment process with clarity on what's involved, how it works and roles and responsibilities. Here's an example thinker assessment form that a coaching custodian can adapt to meet their organisational needs:

### ⏻ Thinker assessment form

**What coaching is** [the organisation's definition] [to be completed by the coaching custodian]

**How it works** [the organisation's definition] [to be completed by the coaching custodian]

**Roles and responsibilities** [coaching custodian, sponsor, line manager, coach, thinker, others] [to be completed by the coaching custodian]

**About the coaching programme** [to be completed by the coaching sponsor]
  » What type of coaching is required (business led, developmental, goal led or programme led)?
  » What's the coaching need for the individual, team and/ or organisation?
  » What's important about this from the organisation's perspective?
  » What's the measure of success that you hope this coaching will lead to?

» What's the anticipated return on the coaching investment?
» What timescales need to be observed? Are there any relevant milestones within that period?
» Is this the best timing for the coaching, based on the annual rhythm of the organisation/role?
» What's the thinker's tenure in the role (transitioning into a new role or well established)?
» What upcoming changes in the organisational structure might impact the coaching or the timing?
» What other demands might the thinker be drawn into that would detract from or alter the coaching?
» Does the organisation's culture support coaching as an intervention?
» How supportive of coaching is the line manager and how prepared are they to make changes to enable the coaching to be successful?
» What has preceded this coaching engagement and what progress has been made as a result?

**About the thinker** [to be completed by the thinker]
» Have you been coached before? If so, how was that experience for you? And the outcomes?
» What's your personal and professional desired outcome from this coaching?
» What makes you consider a coach to support you with this outcome?
» On a scale of 1–10, where 10 is extremely high, how motivated are you to engage with the thinking that will be required of you in coaching?
» Which stage of change do you see yourself at with regard to this outcome [pre-contemplation, contemplation, preparation, action, maintenance]?
» On a scale of 1–10, where 10 is extremely high, how motivated are you to achieve a positive result?

» What's the business case for investing in coaching towards this outcome?

» Describe the coping mechanisms you've used in the past when faced with adversity?

» Think of an example of a time you received some unexpected feedback, something you weren't aware of. How did you respond?

» How have you historically chosen people to support and challenge you in your work?

» What's your preferred learning style(s) that you go to first (taking action, reflecting, researching models that explain a situation, experimentation)?

» On a scale of 1–10, where 10 is extremely high, how much agency do you feel you have for:
  • managing and prioritising your time for learning and growth?
  • seeking regular detailed feedback from multiple sources and then acting upon it?
  • planning the learning opportunities required to get to where you want to be?
  • stretching yourself with practical experiences that will speed your development?
  • networking and joining forces to solve your and others' problems?
  • recognising and responding to new learning needs as they arise?
  • your future career moves?

» What might get in the way of you moving towards your ideal outcome? How might you get in your own way?

» What health or personal circumstances might impact the coaching?

» What do you see as the consequences of success and of missed opportunities with regard to your desired outcome?

The output of screening the thinker and the organisation is a coaching brief that will form the basis of matching to an appropriate coach and briefing them on the potential assignment. See below for an example of a coach briefing document. The next chapter will look at the matching process.

## ↻ Coaching brief (to be shared with the matched coach)

| | |
|---|---|
| Thinker's name | |
| Organisation | |
| Job title | |
| Contact details | E:<br>T: |
| Function/practice group | |
| Line manager | |
| Coaching sponsor | |
| Tripartite meeting required? | Y/N |
| Number of sessions/hours | |
| Fee/expenses | |
| Background and context | |
| Preliminary coaching outcomes | |
| Preliminary coaching measures of success | |
| Learning preference | taking action, reflecting, researching models that explain a situation, experimentation |
| Stage of change | pre-contemplation, contemplation, preparation, action, maintenance |
| Self-directed learner? | Y/N |
| Health issues that might have a bearing (if not confidential) | |
| Chemistry/intro required? | Y/N |

# A word to coaches

Assuming that you're working in an organisational setting (or through an associate company or coaching platform), everything we've discussed about screening *should*, in theory, be part of the coaching custodian's role. We've outlined the process that we'd like these custodians to follow to make the start of your coaching relationship more robust and set up for success. But what happens if no one is taking responsibility for this in the organisations within which you offer coaching?

We see four options, but to help you decide which way to go, find someone you can talk this through with, ideally in supervision with a supervisor who has an organisational background and understands the ramifications for this context:

1. Refuse to work with that organisation!
2. Offer some consultancy to support the coaching custodian in putting processes in place that will enhance the efficacy of the coaching they provide.
3. Ask the coaching custodian some probing questions that they might otherwise not have explored.
4. Create your own checklist and/or process flow to inform your first conversation with the potential thinker.

We suspect that the first option won't be your favourite, as you're continually building a business and want the work. But perhaps it's worth checking in with yourself about what your values say to you about working in such a system where the screening is outsourced to you. And what's the integrity of this piece of work?

You may wish to choose a phase-gated approach – a term taken from project management methodology, sometimes known as a waterfall approach (Chao et al 2005), whereby this screening needs to have happened before you move to a chemistry call. You might feel more inclined to decline this work if/when your pipeline of work is more secure. Or you may have been burned in the past and feel that it isn't worth the potential hassle of having no screening process in place. These are two good reasons for saying 'no thank you' and walking away.

Depending on the extent of the coaching infrastructure that's in place within the organisation, you may decide to propose a consultancy project whereby you support the coaching custodian to do the heavy lifting of devising systems and processes to enhance the efficacy of the coaching. This is worth considering if this is within your skillset.

If you decide you'd simply like to educate the coaching custodian on the answers that you need to do your best work on their behalf, you might ask them the following questions – and you might even insist that they have a conversation with the thinker to establish the answers rather than guessing. We know from the field of Human Centered Design (originated by Professor John E Arnold, Stanford University Design School, 1958) that senior leaders often think they know what others in an organisation want and need, but when we speak to the employees, they want and need something totally different. So, it's important that this doesn't become guesswork on the part of the coaching custodian and that they've had an in-depth conversation with the potential thinker before approaching you.

* What's the reason for asking for coaching for this person?
* How does this coaching fit with the business strategy?
* What's the thinker's understanding of coaching (what it is, what it isn't)?
* How bought into coaching is the thinker? Are they being pushed into it or do they want it?
* How ready for change is the thinker?
* How clear is the thinker on their role in the coaching partnership and that this will require some deep thinking on their part?
* And any other questions you wish to lift from the previous section on screening.

If you're unable or unwilling to challenge the coaching custodian on the questions above, you could use the same set of questions yourself in an introductory call with the thinker. They might be a little leading, though, and they might not get to the truth, the whole truth and nothing but the truth.

## Summary

While this chapter is mostly about the role of the coaching custodian, it is beholden on us coaches as a community to hold coaching custodians to account for their responsibilities in making coaching as successful for their organisation as possible. You might wish to decline that invitation, but think about it this way: your coaching partnerships will be more fulfilling as you get to work with people whose issues are a good fit for coaching, who want coaching and who are willing to do the work that coaching requires of them.

We hope that we have given you ample templates that you can share with the coaching custodians in the organisations where you work, to encourage them to play their part in this win–win–win–win (for them, for the organisation, for you and for the thinker). And don't forget that supervision can support you in this quest to raise standards across the board.

## Reflective practice

* What do *you* believe about pre-screening for coaching readiness?
* Which of your values are showing up (or even being triggered) as you read this chapter? What does that tell you?
* What will you ask for and from whom? Which of these boundaries are non-negotiable and in which circumstances might you flex?
* What's the one thing you'll commit to experiment with that will make a marginal gain in the coaching readiness of the people with whom you work?

# Chapter 4

## Matching through a coaching readiness lens

*Written in collaboration with Sam Humphrey*

### What's required for the matching to happen?

Matching is a critical success factor in any coaching assignment. Assuming the work has been done to identify the coaching need and anticipated success measures, and assuming that the coaching custodian has a pool of competent coaches and the thinker is in a place of readiness for coaching, matching is the next step in setting up a successful coaching assignment.

We're still focused here on coaching within organisations. Chapter 5 covers self-funded coaching.

Matching demands a robust process to ensure integrity in how coaching work is allocated and in preserving the organisation's principles around equality, diversity and inclusion. We suggest that you influence coaching custodians to give their active attention to how they match.

**Understanding the reasons why you've been selected as a possible coach and asking for a clear brief on the coaching assignment are reasonable requests.**

As a professional coach, you might be asked to give up time for chemistry meetings (at no cost if you are external), but it's not a good use of your time, or the thinker's for that matter, to turn up unbriefed and unclear on why you're deemed to be a potential good fit to work together.

Most organisations ask their preferred pool of coaches to prepare a bio that can be used for matching. Whatever the format, the intention at this stage is to enable a sift of the potential coaches and identify which of them can meet the coaching brief.

Why are we including this in a book about coachability? Because, once again, this is all part of creating the best coaching experience possible for the thinker and, at this stage, ensuring that the match enables the thinker to bring their whole self to coaching.

## What is the matching process?

The purpose of matching is to secure the best coach/thinker combination to deliver the coaching work identified at an earlier stage. This process is driven by the coaching brief, which should identify the requirements of the coaching and the coach.

Most organisations conduct some form of matching a thinker with a potential coach(es). This *should* happen prior to a chemistry meeting but it often isn't completed with clarity or purpose, leaving coach and thinker vague as to what they need to cover in a chemistry meeting.

**It's useful for the coaching custodian to be clear on their overall matching process to ensure they involve the right people with the right capabilities at the right time.**

Questions you might encourage coaching custodians to consider include:

1.  *Do they want the thinker to be involved in any of the matching process before the chemistry meeting? If so, how will they brief them on their role and equip them to carry it out well?*

    There's no right or wrong answer to this question. The main benefits of involving the thinker in the pre-chemistry stage are the level of ownership and choice they experience over the process, thus building their agency. The main downside is the time required for the thinker to perform this activity for themselves when looking across a large pool of possible coaches.

    If the thinker is to be involved at an early stage, the coaching custodian should be urged to consider how they plan to ensure that the thinker will have a logical, reasonable and fair approach rather than one that relies on unconscious or unchecked biases. A checklist with clear criteria will minimise these risks and enable a consistency of process.

We know that some organisations and coaching platforms do leave the thinker to choose from a website full of prospective coaches, maybe with filtering options to help them to whittle down what might feel like a daunting number of coaches. This can be a more cost- and time-efficient process.

We don't generally recommend early involvement of the thinker in the matching process, as they're rarely well equipped to conduct this activity though it will give them choice and a sense of their own agency. The coaching custodian will hold knowledge and experience of the coaching pool and is therefore best placed to match possible coaches with the requirements of the coaching.

2. *What's the intended purpose of the chemistry meeting?*

Chemistry meetings often conflate several purposes, because the pre-screening and matching stages leading up to it haven't been properly executed. We're sure you've experienced the 'kitchen sink' purpose of a chemistry meeting – educating the thinker on what coaching is/ isn't, exploring what they might get from being coached, identifying the coaching goal, setting out the coaching process, answering questions about your skill and competence as a coach and then selling yourself as the best coach for them. These types of 'kitchen sink' meetings aren't a good use of anyone's time; there's no guarantee that the thinker will make a good decision and the coaching relationship is set up on potentially inauthentic foundations because the meeting tried to cover too much in too short a time.

**If the pre-screening and matching are in place and have been executed thoroughly, the chemistry meeting has a single purpose – determining compatibility** (see Chapter 7).

3. *Is there a minimum or maximum number of potential coaches that the custodian wants to make available for the chemistry meeting?*

Similar to the above, there's no correct answer to this question, rather a need to consider what will be the best fit for the coaching programme and thinker. This could range from the thinker being assigned a coach to being given a choice of three coaches.

The answer to this question is an important one for coaches because chemistry meetings are often unpaid (for external coaches) yet eat up time (for both internal and external coaches).

**Good pre-screening and matching negate the need for thinkers to meet several coaches.**

We'd argue that a thinker need only meet the one coach who best fits the needs of the coaching assignment. The chemistry meeting would then be focused on both coach and thinker deciding if/how they'll work together.

We suspect that many coaching custodians believe that a 'beauty parade' of two or three coaches is best practice but we contest this perspective. Given that the quality of the coach/thinker relationship is so important in the success of the coaching, we agree that it's vital that the thinker has a choice in who they work with. We also think it's worth reminding the coaching custodian that choice doesn't require the thinker to be involved in every step of the screening or to conduct numerous chemistry meetings because ultimately the thinker makes the decision about whether or not they want to work with a coach. This decision is the one that they're best qualified to make, and they're the only person who can make it. Yet they can meet with one coach, make a decision one way or the other, and if the first doesn't feel like a good fit for them personally, then they can be matched with another coach for a second chemistry session until they're satisfied they've found a compatible match.

4. *Is there a different approach based on the type of coaching?*

We suspect that assigning a coach to a thinker is most acceptable when the coaching being offered is part of a learning programme. This would involve the coaching custodian (or programme lead) providing a team of coaches to work with a programme cohort. If the thinkers are invited to meet two or three coaches and choose who they want to work with, it can become a logistical nightmare and a huge waste of time. It might also result in some coaches having too many thinkers to work with and others too few. We remind the coaching custodian that once they've sifted through the preferred supplier pool for appropriate coaches for this work, the only issue is one of compatibility. We could make the same argument for all types of coaching (business-driven, individual development needs and goal-led coaching). This is not just for efficiency's sake, but for the reasons we've laid out above around choice still being available when a thinker meets one coach, then only meeting another if they don't feel there's a good fit.

5. *Is matching different for internal coaches?*

Before answering this question, the coaching custodian needs to be clear on what purpose they want internal coaches to play in the coaching offer. Do they want to have an internal coaching pool that mirrors the external coaching pool? If so, the same rules will apply to matching internal coaches. In fact, we would strongly argue that where internal coaches are delivering the same type of coaching as externals, they should be subject to all the conditions an external coach must satisfy – training, supervision, insurance, etc.

When matching internal coaches, the main and important difference the coaching custodian needs to be mindful of is the potential for there to be an increased risk of conflict of interest. Internal coaches have non-coaching relationships and reputations within the organisation that may have a bearing on who they can be matched with, and navigating these can be challenging.

When I (Clare) first started coaching, I was working inside an organisation. Coaching was my passion project. There was no coaching custodian in the organisation for which I worked. I simply offered my services to my colleagues. Back then, I didn't understand the importance of working with people outside my immediate function, to avoid any conflicts of interest and give them a sense of confidentiality. They also knew me as the leadership development expert, so would often be looking for advice rather than being willing to find their own answers.

I was looking to practice, so I coached anyone who would have me, no matter how many difficulties around coachability that it created for me and for them. Being willing to coach these people didn't make us the best match – but rather the only match. Still, it was voluntary on their part – they got to choose whether or not to work with me as their coach. But given how well they knew me, they may have felt guilty about discontinuing coaching when they were no longer (or ever) getting value from it. This was compounded by the fact that we didn't contract for a set number of sessions. I was offering coaching ad infinitum. This didn't create a good container for the work and would've made it even harder for us to define an end point. As I look back, I know now that I wasn't paying enough attention to screening, matching or drawing out their agency. I had too much of a vested interest in getting the hours under my belt towards my first level of credential. That's not partnership!

In this chapter we've focused on matching within an organisational context and associate work, and the influence that a coach might have in that arena.

We recognise the rise of the coaching platform, whereby the coach's biography is uploaded onto a platform for the thinker to make a decision about who to work with, often bypassing a chemistry meeting. To this end, coaches might ask themselves how this and other parts of the particular coaching platform set-up align with their values around setting up coaching for success through screening, matching, relationship, agency and reciprocal choice.

As we said previously in Chapter 4, if you're an external coach, you have a choice about which organisations you work with. As an internal coach, you hopefully have some influence over the internal matching processes that the coaching custodian puts in place. Whether you're external or internal, speak up for what you believe works best for coaching readiness, coachability and agency.

# Summary

We've seen how much of the work can be done before the coach is involved to set up the thinker for success and to ensure that they're coaching ready. The coaching experience is more than the programme of coaching itself.

There are a couple more chapters about screening for coaching readiness where no organisation is involved, before moving into enhancing coaching readiness.

## Reflective practice

* What do *you* believe about matching for coaching readiness?
* Which of your values are showing up (or even being triggered) as you read this chapter? What does that tell you?
* What will you ask for and from whom? Which of these boundaries are non-negotiable and in which circumstances might you flex?
* What's the one thing you'll commit to experiment with that will make a marginal gain in the coaching readiness of the people with whom you work?

# Chapter 5

## Referrals through a coaching readiness lens

### Screening those who self-refer for coaching

We've covered a lot of ground about screening and matching within organisations, expectations that we might also apply to associate work and coaching platforms.

Yet you'll be thinking that coaches don't only work through organisations, associate companies or coaching platforms. You may also contract directly with individuals. That might take a different kind of screening, but the principles are the same. You know from the fact that they've approached you that the individual is willing to step into some kind of talking relationship *and* you still need to have a conversation with the individual about whether:

* coaching is the best-fit intervention for their needs (see Chapter 2 on signs and signals)
* they're willing to put in the hard work of thinking and changing (see Chapter 5 and the Appendix on pre-chemistry communication)
* you're compatible (see Chapter 7) to work together.

All of this should happen before you contract with them for the work (Chapter 8).

As part of my screening process, I've started to be more explicit about the people I *don't* work with so that they can self-select out of coaching before we even get to an initial meeting. It saves them time and it saves me time. Feel free to copy this concept, though the words will be led by who you are and aren't as a coach.

## ✪ Why I don't work with just anyone

» I'm not a performance coach.
» I don't do the job that a line manager should be doing, enabling you to be better at your job.
» I don't do the job of a trainer, teaching you how-tos.
» I'm not a mentor, sharing my experiences.

If any of those are what you're looking for, I'm not the person for you.

So, what do I do, then, as a leadership and transitions coach?

I work with you to identify who you are, what's important to you, what you want to be known for, how you want to show up, and what you want and need to jettison to become the person and leader you wish to be.

That means you need to be willing to go there – to explore your true north and move away from whatever's holding you back from reaching your full potential as a human being rather than a human doing.

If you're not ready to contemplate what matters most to you and to make some changes in the way you work and live to align with what matters most, I don't want to take your or your company's money.

I don't have a magic wand (nor magical answers), but I do have powerful questions that will help you to identify what you want from the next chapter of your life and to go after that – if that's what you want (not what your boss wants, your partner wants, or your parents want...).

To be sure that we start as we mean to go on, in a worthwhile partnership, I'll ask you some searching questions about your goals and intentions for yourself, your work and this coaching.

I expect that you'll probe me too, to ensure that we're a

good fit for your learning and thinking styles.

This will be a mutual agreement to work together, matching your desire to become more of the human you wish to be with my very human coaching skills.

Only then, once we've decided that this is a relationship that can work for us both, will we sketch out how to work together to get the most from the coaching, given all that we know about each other.

Be prepared for a state of deepening awareness.

This concept of describing who you *don't* work with is just as important as defining who you *do* work with. This self-screening means that you get to have initial chemistry conversations only with those people who qualify themselves as being willing and able to step into this way of working. You may think this cuts down on your leads – and yes, it does. But it means that you have fewer unqualified leads with whom to have an initial no-cost chemistry session.

**I'd rather have a smaller funnel of better qualified leads than a larger funnel of unqualified and ultimately non-qualifying leads.**

My thanks to William Buist for this idea, which is serving me well.

## How to educate referrers about coaching readiness

Sometimes you'll get referrals from people you've coached before or other people in your network who know and love you. That's very gratifying and it cuts down on your business development time and effort. But sometimes, these referrers might send people your way who aren't coaching ready, or someone for whom you're not the best match as coach. Just because you and the referrer worked well together doesn't necessarily mean that you and their friend or colleague will be compatible.

And just because you are good at something doesn't mean that you want to spend your time in that way. I've had a few people referred to me for work that the referrer knows I have the skills to do, but perhaps they don't realise that I don't have the will. When I've gone ahead with the work, it hasn't been fulfilling for me (and I suspect that leaks out to the thinker, too).

If these referrals are within an organisation where you have a coaching contract (or would like one), you'll need to speak with the coaching custodian to check that this is right for the organisation.

Whether coaching is through an associate company or self-funded, it's worth getting really clear about who you do and don't work with, what people can expect from working with you, how they'll need to step into the space to make the most from it, and why you adhere to a certain set of boundaries (whatever your boundaries are). That way, if you have champions who frequently send people to you, you can have a conversation with them and/or send them information that will help them to send good matches to you. You could also include this information when you ask thinkers at the end of a coaching programme for referrals.

Of course, you can and will still personally screen the prospective thinker yourself to be sure that they and what they want help with are a good fit for coaching and that you're a good match for each other. Think about this as part of the whole coaching experience. Marketers and salespeople would call these referrals qualified. Your prospect qualification process might include more than coaching readiness, but that's beyond the scope of this book. **Qualified prospects still need screening for coaching readiness and compatibility.**

# Summary

Referrals will always be an important part of your coaching pipeline. I encourage you to figure out ways to get better qualified referrals ahead of your first meeting, whether those are self-referrals or referrals from your network. Be clear about the types of people you wish to work with and how you work, including how they will get the most out of coaching. Pre-screening is vital for all concerned.

## Reflective practice

* What do *you* believe about referrals and self-referral in relation to coaching readiness?
* Which of your values are showing up (or even being triggered) as you read this chapter? What does that tell you?
* What will you ask for and from whom? Which of these boundaries are non-negotiable and in which circumstances might you flex?
* What's the one thing you'll commit to experiment with that will make a marginal gain in the coaching readiness of the people with whom you work?

# Chapter 6

# Communication through a coaching readiness lens

In Chapter 1, I talked about the importance of the whole thinker experience, from start to finish. Communications before and in between meetings are all part of that thinker experience and need to be thought through carefully, particularly in terms of preparing the thinker to be coaching ready. **Think of your communications as warming them up to be present, enhancing their engagement to wring the most value out of the coaching.**

You may wish to use a version of the questions in Chapter 1 to enable a prospective thinker to have another opportunity to:

* ❋ understand what will make coaching more impactful for them personally
* ❋ self-select in or out of coaching, knowing full well what they're responsible for.

I've repurposed those questions in the Appendix, and you can also download these from my website to make them your own.

What else do you need to pay attention to in your written communications with the thinkers with whom you work, whether that's upfront or in between sessions? How will you keep fostering more agency in them? Which words and phrases invite them into thinking for themselves?

We'll look at pre-session preparation questions for the thinker and post-session reflection questions in Chapters 10 and 12 respectively.

**As much as you pay attention to how to increase their agency through your way of being, also think about what *undermines* their agency.** For example, inviting them to report back on their progress in between sessions (unless they explicitly ask for this, in which case get them to write it in an email so they can use the time you're together to get to new thinking). This isn't a teacher/student relationship where you check their homework (see Shifts 70 and 73 in *The Transformational Coach*). That makes them the Child to your Parent, diminishing their agency.

## Reflective practice

❋ What do *you* believe about written communications in relation to coaching readiness?

❋ Which of your values are showing up (or even being triggered) as you read this (granted, very short) chapter? What does that tell you?

❋ What will you ask for and from whom? Which of these boundaries are non-negotiable and in which circumstances might you flex?

❋ What's the one thing you'll commit to experiment with that will make a marginal gain in the coaching readiness of the people with whom you work?

# Chapter 7

## Coaching compatibility through a coaching readiness lens

*Written in collaboration with Sam Humphrey*

### What's the purpose of a chemistry session?

Based on the numerous chemistry meetings you've conducted and what you've found to work for you, you probably have a chemistry groove you fall into. You may have a well-practised format or script you apply to put yourself in prime position to win the client. Our intention in this chapter is to bounce you out of your unconscious competence and offer some provocations to help you consciously think about how you approach a chemistry meeting and how you can best prepare for it.

The term chemistry is often used when people are speaking about dating. People talk about a couple having great chemistry, no chemistry or sexual chemistry. It's for this reason that we think this term should be dislodged from the coaching lexicon and replaced with a more professional and less emotive word that better describes the purpose of this meeting. More on that later in the chapter.

What's the purpose of a chemistry meeting? Our experience has shown us that the purpose of these meetings has become confused and multipurpose. If thinkers haven't been exposed to a thorough set-up and screening process, chemistry meetings can often require coaches to satisfy several purposes, including:

* a 'teach-in' where they explain what coaching is and isn't
* a thinker screen to assess if the thinker is coaching ready
* an outcome discussion to understand what the thinker wants

from coaching and whether coaching is the most appropriate intervention for that outcome

✳ a sales pitch where the coach has to prove to the thinker that they're the best person to coach them.

On the basis that this first meeting with a thinker is what will determine whether you continue the work or not, it seems vitally important that the set-up and purpose of this is clear, so asking the coaching custodian for clarity would be a smart move.

Our view is that if a coaching assignment is well set up, as described in the previous chapters, then a chemistry meeting need be no more or less than a compatibility meeting between you and the thinker. The purpose of the meeting can then focus on both of you deciding whether you can work together and exploring any extenuating circumstances that might interfere with your work, such as being a good friend of the thinker's partner or a shareholder in the thinker's organisation.

The idea that there needs to be some magical energy between coach and thinker detracts from the reality of the working world, where relationships are never perfect. **Coaching can provide a learning laboratory for working with imperfection.**

We know that people often have to find a way to work with others with whom they may or may not have chosen to work alongside. Beginning a new relationship with a coach provides a live learning platform for the thinker to explore how they build effective working relationships. What do they do that works or doesn't? How can they accelerate those actions? What could they try out or experiment with? Awareness of this means they can transplant this learning and improve the quality and effectiveness of their existing working relationships.

In this context, the question the chemistry meeting needs to answer is this: are there any reasons why you and the thinker couldn't work well together? This is quite a shift from the traditional context for a chemistry meeting where the question is 'Do I like/get on with this coach more or less than the other coach(es)?' The former question demands you and the thinker to enquire, be curious and engage from the get-go. In contrast, the latter question demands that you please and entertain, to be the most popular. We'd suggest that the former sits more comfortably in the realm of professional coaching as the latter is potentially fraught with bias and superficiality and is open to abuse.

How do you best prepare for a chemistry meeting? This is a question we sometimes hear thinkers ask but hear less frequently from experienced coaches. You'll almost certainly have had more experience of chemistry meetings than thinkers and most likely have developed a format or outline.

We suggest that you approach chemistry meetings with a renewed outlook that speaks to the inquisitive nature of good coaching. We also recommend that you encourage the coaching custodian to approach the set-up of a chemistry meeting in a similar way to the set-up of a job interview.

Job interviews must comply with legal requirements so that the process is fair to all and doesn't discriminate on grounds of race, religion, ethnicity, age, gender, etc. Interviews are also set up to elicit comparable data to allow fair and effective decision making. If you compare a job interview to a chemistry meeting, the interviewer (akin to the thinker in our context) will typically have some training, or at least a briefing, about how to conduct an interview. The selection criteria will be clear and explicit, and the interviewer will be given a set of questions to ask each candidate to ensure consistency. The candidate (the coach) knows what the job is (the coaching brief) and that they meet the minimum require-ments of the job. They may have sight of the interview criteria and can prepare their answers in advance. They'll also come with their own set of due diligence questions that will help them decide whether they want to accept the job if it's offered to them.

Applying this interview mindset to a chemistry meeting highlights the need for objectivity to ensure the meeting has integrity and is fair to all. Organisations and coaches who are serious about equality, diversity and inclusion must ensure they give attention to all their people practices and policies, including this one.

## What's in a name: chemistry or compatibility?

We've looked at how chemistry sessions have, over time, become more than about establishing fit, often squeezing out this critical element of the meeting: can coach and thinker see themselves working together? **We'd like to propose a new name for the chemistry session to make it even more obvious what *this* meeting is about: the compatibility meeting.**

According to the *Cambridge Dictionary*, compatibility is 'being able to exist, live, or work successfully with something or someone else'. In the case of coaching, can coach and thinker work together successfully?

This isn't just about gut feeling (though our instinct often plays a part and we ignore it at our peril). Coaching requires the coach to coach well and it requires the thinker to think well – to be coaching ready. Take account of equality, diversity and inclusion as you first meet people. They may be different from you, but that doesn't make them uncoachable by you or that someone else is better suited to their needs. Be aware of how you feel about differences, explore areas that are similar and different and reflect together on what impact that might have on the coaching (see Shift 37 in *The Transformational Coach*).

As an aside, this is the only place in this book that the word 'uncoachable' is used, though you'll notice that we use it to say that a person is *not* uncoachable. Generally, you or another coach can support a person to trust themselves to think, but it does take two to tango, with them leading this dance – as long as it's a dance that's suited to coaching.

What's the data that you personally look out for when you first meet a potential thinker? Maybe it's about how they respond to challenge. And remember that the thinker will become more coachable than they might at first present, as you encourage that muscle to build.

This is the coach and thinker's initial meeting together where you'll get your first inklings about their unique blend of coaching readiness and how to draw it forth. **You can't pour coachability in; together, though, you can entice it out, cultivating it as you go.**

We refer you back to the signs and signals of coaching readiness in Chapter 2, particularly where you're working directly with a self-referred individual who hasn't been through a preliminary organisational screening.

At every step of the coaching journey, look out for coaching readiness and its contraindications and support the thinker to become more coachable than they might at first appear. If they've never had coaching before, you'd hope that the coaching custodian has explained how it works in theory, but they may still have little idea about how to show up in practice in a way that gets the most out of coaching. It's the coach's role to support them in growing into this.

Even if they've had coaching before, it may be different from the kind of coaching that you offer, and they may behave in ways that don't make the most of this coaching offering. Meet them where they are every step of the way, and start as you mean to go on, with a compatibility session that has coaching readiness in mind and also knowing that neuroplasticity is possible, no matter what the age and stage of a potential thinker.

## Preparation for the coach

Here are some questions for you, the coach, to help you think about your beliefs and methods more consciously, and to prepare for each compatibility meeting.

## ⟨⟩ Compatibility call preparation for the coach

» What's the purpose of this meeting? Is it purely about compatibility or are you wrapping other intentions into it? And does this muddy the water?

» What logistical points need to be in place?
   • location for privacy and therefore the ability to talk candidly
   • duration of the meeting, given the purpose
   • understanding the follow-up process after the meeting, especially if this is an organisational contract and not your own process.

» If screening hasn't been done by the organisation, what are *your* criteria to determine whether the potential thinker is a good match at this time for coaching? (See also Chapter 2, 'Signs and signals'). Including but not limited to:
   • conflicts of interest
   • whether they appear to be self-absorbed and blaming others, closed minded or resistant to change
   • whether the coaching stems from unaddressed performance management issues
   • timing of the coaching for the individual
   • whether they want and/or feel the need for coaching.

» What are your criteria to determine compatibility with a potential thinker? This isn't about whether you get on, as this isn't about friendship.
   • What's your style of coaching, and do they appear to be ready for that? How will you test this out in the compatibility session?
   • What are your values and which opposing values would stop you from working with someone?
   • Which kinds of organisations do you choose

to work with or not (for example, the tobacco industry, gambling, pornography). You'd usually know this before a compatibility meeting, but it can sometimes take you by surprise.

- If you have a political stance, what issues might that throw up for you while working with someone of a different political persuasion?
- If you have a faith, what issues might arise in working with people of alternative faiths?

» Who do you work best with?

» Who do you not work well with?

» How do you need to present yourself to ensure you can both determine if you're compatible?

» How can you prime yourself before the meeting so you can show up as you want to?

» What mindset do you wish to adopt as you step into the coaching?

## Preparation for the thinker

You also want the thinker to arrive fully prepared to have an informed compatibility conversation. Too often, they don't know what to expect of this kind of meeting and attend without having thought through what they want from a coaching relationship.

You can support them to get ready by sending them a version of this set of questions. Once again, this is a suite of options. Once you know what you're looking for by way of compatibility and how you'll structure the meeting (see below), you can choose the questions that best reflect your position.

### ↻ Compatibility call preparation for the thinker

The purpose of our upcoming call is to establish whether we're compatible to work together. To this end, I encourage you to think about the following questions ahead of time. Please know that everything we talk about in this session will be confidential, except in the following circumstances:

» I'm concerned for your or others' safety.
» I'm concerned that you have or are about to commit child abuse, treason, money laundering or acts of terrorism.
» I'm required by law to share information.

In each case, I'll talk this through directly with you first, except where this is prescribed by law or where your safety may be at immediate risk as a result of such disclosure. Please note that as my contract will be with your organisation, we will also be jointly bound by the organisation's code of conduct.

» What has brought you to coaching?
» What time and resources are you willing to dedicate to making change happen for yourself through the coaching process?
» What's your hope for this meeting?
» How will you know it has been a successful meeting for you?
» What are you looking for in a coach?
» What are you not looking for in a coach?
» How do you feel about being coached by a [insert your own intersectionalities, such as race, gender, class, religion, political affiliation, etc]? What does a coach need to bear in mind while working with you if you're of a different race, class, religion, political affiliation, ability, thinking style?
» What kind of support and challenge do you want from your coach? How can we enable you to draw out your best thinking?
» What criteria will you use to determine our compatibility – positive and contraindications?
» Based on other fruitful working relationships you've had in the past, what was your contribution and what

was the other's contribution that you can apply to these criteria?

» Based on unsuccessful/suboptimal working relationships you've had in the past, what was your contribution and what was the other's contribution that you can apply to these criteria?

» Which of these criteria can you only check out in this meeting?
  • If credibility of the coach is important to you, check this out through other sources first [insert links to your LinkedIn, bio, website, etc].

» How do you need to present yourself to ensure we can determine whether we're compatible?

» What do you need to ask your coach to prepare in advance of the meeting? For example, you might want to ask the coach:
  • What's your philosophy of coaching?
  • When and who do you coach at your best?
  • What experience do you have of coaching people like me?
  • How do you maintain your professional development as a coach?
  • What boundary issues have you encountered and how did you deal with them?
  • How will you work with me on my learning goals?

[These questions – from Clutterbuck (2020) – may or may not be important to you, but they may give you some ideas about the kinds of things you may wish to ask].

So, you've prepared yourself and primed the potential thinker. Now it's time to have the compatibility meeting. But for how long and how will you structure it?

# Structure of the compatibility meeting

In our experience, most chemistry sessions last between 30 and 45 minutes, but they're trying to squeeze a lot into that short time. We believe that 30–45 minutes is optimal for the meeting when compatibility is the main purpose, alongside double-checking their coaching readiness. Research (Berry et al 2011) suggests that there's no difference between coaching outcomes from face-to-face and virtual coaching and we experience the same for compatibility meetings.

We suggest the following structure (though please assess these items with your own values and beliefs in mind):

## ☉ Compatibility meeting structure

Invite them to be themselves – this is a safe place to bring their visible and invisible differences. Set out the purpose of the meeting and get an agreement over it being about compatibility. Restate the confidentiality (and exceptions) of everything that's said in this meeting and any future meetings.

**Establish that this is a mutual decision-making process whereby you both get the opportunity to choose whether to work together or not.**

With a mindset of curiosity and humanity, ask them:

» what it's like for them to be meeting with you [or different coaches if this is part of a 'beauty parade' process] and starting on this journey [acknowledging whatever they say]

» how they'll assess the success or otherwise of this meeting once it's over

» about themselves:

- What makes your heart sing?
- Who does your work and life serve? Who else? Who else?
- If we have a chair for every one of those people, what would they be saying? (Peter Hawkins, podcast

with Clare Norman and Steve Ridgley, 2021)
» about their end in mind for the coaching itself:
  - If we do decide to work together, how would you know that it has been useful for you in six to nine months' time? What would you be seeing, hearing, feeling that would tell you that this coaching had been worthwhile for you?
  - And what would other people notice about you? How would they experience you differently that would make a difference to your life and work?
» what their understanding is of coaching and how it can support and challenge them with these hopes and intentions
» how they do their best thinking and how you can support and challenge them in that (given that this is all about their thinking, not the coach's)
» about examples where they have made changes to their life and work in the past and how they have gone about that
» for their thoughts on the coaching readiness questions (see the Appendix) and how they might enhance some of their self-assessments with your support in order to get the most out of coaching
» how they might activate themselves between sessions to experiment
» what structures they need to put in place to enable them to get the most out of coaching – both in sessions and between
» how things might go wrong between you and how they would wish to work through that
» whether there's anything you should know about them, such as past history, illnesses, medication, therapy, recent bereavements, sleep patterns, which might have an influence on the way they think
» what questions they have for you.

Even this is a lot for 30–45 minutes! So please use the above, not as a checklist so much as a series of choices to make that match with your own values and beliefs about compatibility and agency. During this meeting, listen out for signs and signals of coaching readiness and compatibility.

Give them the option to reflect and talk to other coaches, or tell them immediately if you think there's a reason why the two of you shouldn't work together and discuss how to feed this back to the sponsor – or if they're a private client, how you can help them to find more compatible support for their needs.

# Decision making after the compatibility meeting

The ultimate aim of any compatibility meeting is to enable both the thinker and the coach to decide if they're going to work together. We've covered the importance of ensuring this is an informed decision. Where both parties agree to go ahead, the coaching will move forward and the next steps will be agreed and confirmed.

If the thinker doesn't choose to go ahead with you as coach, this will usually be communicated to you by either the thinker or the coaching custodian. Assuming the purpose of the meeting was clear, you may also be able to elicit some useful feedback about why you weren't chosen.

Where things get riskier is when you as coach don't want to go ahead with the thinker. Feeding this back to the thinker or the coaching custodian is fraught with potential potholes that could not only negatively impact the thinker's career and/or their self-esteem but also your future contractual engagement as a coach within their organisation.

Listen to your gut for what Robert Biswas-Diener (2023) calls yellow lights – cautionary indicators. He treats yellow lights as red lights when it comes to deciding not to work with someone. This doesn't mean a person isn't worthy of being coached, but there may be very good reason not to proceed. You get to choose just as much as they do.

**In coaching, declining to work with someone you don't think you're a good match for isn't a slight on your professionalism.**

At the same time, you do have a duty of care to feed this back sensitively.

If you have a clear purpose for the compatibility meeting and clarity on the decision-making criteria, it enables you and the thinker to gather relevant data in the meeting, which makes it much easier for you both to explain reasons for not wanting to go ahead with the work.

If the set-up before the meeting hasn't been done well or thoroughly, you may discover that the thinker's objective isn't suited to coaching, that the thinker isn't coaching ready/willing or that the organisation isn't well placed to support the thinker to achieve or maintain their objectives. While all of these would be valid reasons to turn down the coaching assignment, feeding this back to the coaching custodian has the added risk of offending them by pointing out that they haven't done a good job in setting up the coaching for success.

Our recommendation is that, as a coach, you should equip yourself with a process that you can easily deploy to give that feedback and in the short term to plug the gaps in the organisation's set-up.

⭐ You're invited to meet a potential new thinker. The coaching custodian tells you that they're worried about this newly appointed leader. The leader is working extremely hard and doing very well but the custodian is concerned that the leader is going to burn out.

At the compatibility meeting, the thinker immediately confesses that they're stressed. The demands of the new job are challenging but he says he can handle them. The source of the stress is an affair that he's having with a colleague. He's unsure about what to do and doesn't know how to approach this problem. He wants coaching to help him determine his decision-making approach.

There are several ethical and moral issues to be wrestled with in the above scenario, namely:

*Is coaching the appropriate intervention here?*
It could be. Supporting a client to determine decision-making criteria is a common coaching objective. The only difference here is the nature of the decision the client has to make.

*How do I coach someone if I think their behaviour is morally wrong?*
As a coach, you always have a choice over whether to accept or reject a client. Chances are you'll have moral differences with some of your clients, though you rarely see them as they don't come up in your conversations.

*What responsibilities does the coach have in this situation?*
Most coaches don't charge a fee for compatibility meetings, which means that, at that point in time, there's no contract in place, so the rules around confidentiality may be different.

This distinction is important.

When a coach is under contract, they're required to break confidentiality under specific circumstances. In this scenario, there are three points where the coach could be colluding with the thinker and therefore effecting a breach:

» First, with the organisation. Most organisations have a policy about relationships at work and in this scenario, the leader's organisation requires staff to declare work relationships to HR. As the leader hasn't followed this policy, they're technically in breach of the organisation's code of conduct. A coach working with a thinker while knowingly colluding with them around not following the policy would be in breach of their contract with the organisation.

» Second, with the coaching professional body. Most professional bodies require coaches to abide by a code of ethics. A coach knowingly colluding with a client in breach of their contract would be a breach of the terms of their contract and therefore the coaching code of ethics.

» Third, with the organisation's regulatory body. In this scenario, the regulatory body requires that work relationships are declared to protect the organisation's clients' and employees' rights. A coach knowingly working with a thinker in breach of their contract would be effecting another breach.

In managing this scenario, what the coach does next is vital. The appropriate steps are either to agree to work with the client, on the condition that they fulfil their contractual obligations, or to refuse the work.

# Summary

The efficacy of coaching is driven by the relationship between coach and thinker (De Haan 2008), hence the importance of the compatibility meeting. Coach and thinker are deciding whether they wish to proceed. We're beginning to draw out coachability and agency at this stage, but bear in mind that it's an ongoing education process. Not teaching per se, but continually holding the thinker to account for thinking and making changes.

## Reflective practice

* What do *you* believe about chemistry/compatibility meetings in relation to coaching readiness?
* Which of your values are showing up (or even being triggered) as you read this chapter? What does that tell you?
* What will you ask for and from whom? Which of these boundaries are non-negotiable and in which circumstances might you flex?
* What's the one thing you'll commit to experiment with that will make a marginal gain in the coaching readiness of the people with whom you work?

# Chapter 8

## Contracting through a coaching readiness lens

### Big C contracting

As coaches, we all know how important contracting is, so that all parties are in agreement about what the coaching is and is not, logistics (where, when, how often), fees, etc. But coaching isn't just an exchange of a service for payment – it's complex and relational. So the written, formal contract is not enough.

As contracting is part of the whole thinker experience, it's important to construct the contract through a coaching readiness lens: does the contracting help the thinker to come to coaching prepared and ready to think? With agency?

This is where the relationship-building, verbal contracting comes in. In partnering to design the alliance, as Whitworth et al describe it (1998), we're enabling the thinker to have a choice in how the coach and thinker will engage in this work together. Coaching isn't something that they simply show up to and have done unto them, but rather it's co-created in a way that builds their agency. This is a crucial part of empowering them to articulate their needs.

So, alongside discussion about the theme of the coaching, their desired outcomes, their measures of success, what's important to them about that, what's in scope and out of scope (see Shift 2 in *The Transformational Coach*), we must spend time on the relational aspects of the coaching agreement.

Given the importance of relationship in coaching (De Haan 2008), this psychological contract discussion will enable coach and thinker to start the coaching having highlighted potential difficulties in an objective way, before they arise. This puts both parties in 'Adult' mode and enables both to be coaching ready. Here are some suggested questions (adapted from Hawkins & Turner 2020).

* What aspects can we bring into awareness that might otherwise influence the coaching under the surface?
* What as yet unspoken expectation do we have of each other?
* What anxieties or concerns might we each have? What will we do if we uncover something we're concerned about?
* How will we deal with issues of shame regarding sharing of 'mistakes'?
* How might either of us unwittingly sabotage our relationship?
* How might we recover trust if something does go wrong?
* What do we do to prevent potential dependency issues?
* How will we recognise when either of us feels overwhelmed? Or rebellious? Or [insert word that they've used themselves]?
* What ground rules have we agreed to ensure that either one of us will feel comfortable enough to raise issues about our relationship?

Be present to their answers. Discuss and agree. I've written this before, and I'll say it again here: **meet the thinker where they are** – you have time to work together and you can bring out the coachability in them over time. But to set them up for success, keep their agency in mind at every step of the thinker experience. Encourage them to express their needs and be sure to articulate your own boundaries as well.

## Outlining the timeline

The coach can also help the thinker to think better by being clear about the timeline of working together and their respective roles at each stage. **The more the thinker understands about the process, the more they can settle into that process rather than worrying about the unknowns.**

As a coach, you might consider drawing the timeline of the experience so that you both have a visual, such as the one below.

**Starting the coaching process**

Tripartite if organisational coaching.

Thinker preparation: history and vision.

Do you ask them to complete anything about their journey-line for example, or their strengths; what do you ask them about their vision for coaching?

↓

**Just before a coaching session**

Thinker Preparation.

Do you send them a set of questions to get them coaching ready for a session?

↓

**In a coaching session**

● Contract for the work ●

● Explore the territory ●

● What and who ●

● Plan next steps ●

● Close the session with learning ●

↓

**After a session**

Thinker reflections.

Do you send them a set of questions to support their reflections and commitments and to build their agency?

↓

**In-between sessions**

Thinker does the work.

(Could be research, action, thinking, reflection)

↓

**Completing the process**

Tripartite if organisational coaching.

Last session to make a good ending.

What's your process for each of these stages in the coaching experience? How will you offer that lightly to the thinker so that they can ask for something different at this contracting stage if they wish to? This is their coaching, and this is a partnership. Even though you have expertise in holding this kind of process, they have expertise in how they personally learn and grow. Invite them to respond in any way to your skeleton of a process so that they feel empowered to make decisions on their own behalf because this will build their agency and self-efficacy – their coaching readiness.

My thanks to Sue Gravells for her insight about this piece of the puzzle.

## Contracting for mindset

As part of the contracting discussion, re-emphasise that this isn't another work meeting and nor is it a cosy chat. **This is self-development, and it requires a different mindset and rules of engagement to the kind of meeting that the thinker might be used to.**

Discuss how you'll support and challenge them to bring forth the mindsets of agency articulated in the pre-compatibility questionnaire (see the Appendix):

✳ embracing their role as thinker in the coaching process and what this means in practice
✳ moving beyond known thinking to new thinking
✳ being open to challenge
✳ understanding that there's no right answer for the issues they bring to coaching – only answers that fit their unique needs, personality and context
✳ both of you believing that the thinker is 'creative, resourceful and whole'
✳ realising that the thinking will use their head, heart and gut to access new wisdom
✳ experimentation in coaching and outside of it
✳ establishing that real change happens when they focus on

themselves, who they wish to be, not just the problems they need to solve
* the need to work on the system around them to remove barriers.

You might also discuss how they can accelerate and enhance their thinking by considering:

* getting enough sleep to enable them to think clearly
* building in physical activity to their routines to promote their mental acuity
* walking in nature to restore their attention
* eating nutritious food to support critical thinking
* drinking enough water to keep their brain hydrated and at peak thinking capacity
* proactively keeping stress levels under control in whatever ways that work for them
* purposefully using technology so as not to drain their energy.

You'll know from experience that certain logistical elements will support the value they can extract from coaching, so you might also discuss whether they can commit to:

* blocking time on both sides of a coaching session to prepare mentally and physically, and to reflect
* turning up on time, every time
* switching off distractions in the coaching session
* carving out deep thinking time in their diary, over and above their coaching.

As the coach, you know that these aspects will support them to get the most value out of the coaching. Consider how you might have this conversation in a way that is Adult–Adult rather than Parent–Child (using Berne's terms – see Chapter 11). You'll have seen what has worked for thinkers in the past, and therefore have some expertise in this area, but you don't want to strip them of their agency by assuming Parent mode. This might be the only time in coaching that you propose ways in which they can help themselves in the above ways, as you then move towards non-directive coaching.

# Little c contracting

At the start of every coaching session, you'll establish the coaching agreement for this particular session. Once again, this form of contracting gives the power to the thinker to figure out what's important for them to bring to coaching today, relating to their overall coaching goals. This will enhance their agency by enabling them to articulate their needs.

You can read more about this in *The Transformational Coach* (Shifts 3 and 14), but for ease of reference, I'll revisit it here so you can consider how these questions **build the thinking muscles of the thinker and enable them to voice their needs where they may not previously have felt able to express those needs**.

The acronym spells CONTRACT, and there are multiple ways to work through this: it's not meant to be a script, but more a set of guiding principles that start the coaching as you mean to go on – with the thinker in the driving seat. As the coach, you guide the process, and you decide nothing.

# ☉ Session contracting

| **C**heck in | • What's important for us to focus on today? [Only if they wish to talk about their progress since last time, continue with...] What are you learning about yourself since our last session?<br>• I'd like to acknowledge your... |
|---|---|
| **O**bjective | • What would be useful to think about today? [if they didn't already answer this question in answer to the first check-in question] |
| **N**ecessity | • What's important to you about this?<br>• Which of your values does this tap into? |
| **T**ime | • What's your specific question for today's x minutes? |
| **R**ealisation | • How will you know this conversation has been useful for you by the time we finish? |
| **A**genda | • What do we need to cover to get us to that measure of success?<br>• What's in scope and out of scope?<br>• Or, what themes do you anticipate will come up for you during this session?<br>• What are you most curious about regarding this issue? (See Robert Biswas-Diener 2023.) |
| **C**o-creation | • What might prevent us from achieving this goal today?<br>• How shall we partner to move through that?<br>• What strengths, values or strategies can you call on to achieve this session goal?<br>• May I have your permission to interrupt in service of your new thinking? |
| **T**heir agenda | • Where would it be most useful to start? |

As you've seen, contracting is an integral part of setting up the thinker to embrace their full agency. This may feel unfamiliar to them, especially if they've previously relied on others to tell them what to do. It may even feel difficult for them, but it's certainly within their gift to figure out their answers themselves.

# Summary

You know how important contracting is to create boundaries within which the work will take place. This gives both parties a degree of trust in the process and in each other. Psychological safety is part and parcel of coaching readiness. And it's important to consider what to include in these stages of coaching to enhance agency in the thinkers with whom you work.

## Reflective practice

* What do *you* believe about contracting in relation to coaching readiness?
* Which of your values are showing up (or even being triggered) as you read this chapter? What does that tell you?
* What will you ask for and from whom? Which of these boundaries are non-negotiable and in which circumstances might you flex?
* What's the one thing you'll commit to experiment with that will make a marginal gain in the coaching readiness of the people with whom you work?

# Chapter 9

## Three-way contracting through a coaching readiness lens

*Written in collaboration with Sam Humphrey*

In organisational coaching, it's good practice to require the full commitment of the line manager or sponsor to support the thinker on a day-to-day basis. **As coaches, we're not with the thinker every day, so organisational support is vital to continue the momentum between coaching sessions.**

⭐ I (Clare) have to admit that I didn't follow this protocol when I first started coaching inside the corporate that I worked in, because I'd never heard of three-way contracting in my training. Only later did I hear about it and asked for support to figure out how to do it (thank you, Eve Turner, for your generosity). Contracting exclusively with the individual meant that we (the thinkers and I) lost out on organisational recognition for the contribution that coaching was making to the success of its people and the ripple effect on their teams. Even though the organisation was paying our salaries, we also tended to work on personal development goals rather than organisational goals. While I'm all for individuals choosing what they bring to coaching, systemic coaching must pay attention to all stakeholders, including those they lead, colleagues, investors, customers, partners, their local community, plus the wider ecology (Hawkins & Turner 2020) rather than being another version of an employee assistance scheme.

Because the line manager or sponsor is a pivotal support in between coaching sessions, tripartite meetings are useful to set up the coaching for success, addressing all of those stakeholder needs. Coaching readiness can be enhanced by the support of the line manager or sponsor. The tripartite brings the voice of the paying client into the room and lays out all stakeholders' expectations of this process.

There may be exceptions to this practice and coaching custodians will devise their own terms and governance for those exceptions.

# The purpose of the tripartite

All of the aspects below could be the coach or the organisation stating their position or a form of contracting between the three parties – coach, line manager/sponsor and thinker:

* to be clear on the purpose of the coaching – driven by a business need, developmental, goal orientated or programme led
* to agree the confidentiality agreement (how feedback will be managed, when confidentiality will be broken and what the process is for that, harvesting learning/themes across multiple coaching assignments)
* to agree what role the sponsor will play, including setting up another session(s) to gather data about the success/progress of the coaching
* to understand and manage the expectations of the coaching because:

    * change might not immediately be visible
    * movement backwards can be part of the forward change

* to agree how to handle specific issues (for example, if the individual decides they wish to leave the company)
* to agree the outcome of the coaching, which will inform the coaching goals/agenda
* to agree measurement of coaching and/or the thinker (how they'll know it has been achieved, which is an opportunity to

understand what success looks like, not a diagnosis of what the problem is)

✳ to make sure the coaching goals are coaching goals rather than performance/work goals

✳ to agree positive and/or negative consequences

✳ an opportunity to highlight strengths to leverage/amplify/transfer to this work

✳ to be a forward-looking activity

✳ coaching works best alongside other organisational interventions, so what are these and can they be resourced (or this could be done with the coaching custodian)?

✳ to explore any systemic factors that might affect the coaching outcome, such as reorganisation, individuals who block, resources available (using PESTLE, SWOT analysis, McKinsey 7-S, Burke Litwin – see Bibliography), or this could be done with the coaching custodian

✳ pre-existing 360˚ feedback data can play a part in this meeting to inform the goals and measures of success.

Once again, bear in mind that every interaction, every conversation and every piece of communication has an impact on the agency of the thinker. Keep this front and centre as you encourage them to ask questions for clarity and state their own needs. You may wish to add in a preparatory meeting before this one for the thinker to try things on for size, such that they build agency to ask for the things they may never have expressed before.

## What the tripartite is not

✳ a cosy chat without an agenda

✳ a pile-on of everything the thinker does wrong/badly

✳ an opportunity for the sponsor to avoid delivering important feedback/messages in the hope that the thinker will understand by osmosis

✳ solution suggestions – what they need to do is…

* wishy-washy – waffle, vague statements, unclear measurements, dodging the issue
* a performance review or feedback session
* an opportunity to understand a root cause for the purpose of attributing blame
* about the coach and sponsor.

## Who can attend the tripartite?

* the line manager – in our view, this is most valuable because they're closest to the thinker on a day-to-day basis and are responsible for their success
* the thinker
* the coach
* the HR/L&D/talent specialist, though not in lieu of the line manager
* nominated others.

## Notes for the coach in the tripartite

* Encourage the thinker to lead, to build their agency.
* Know your boundaries – what you will and won't agree to do.
* Focus on the outcome and how you'll all know it has been achieved. For example, an HR director once told me (Clare) that a potential thinker needed to become more mature through this process of coaching. How would you recognise maturity? What would this maturity facilitate – that's the real outcome?
* Recognise that people often lead with their judgements, not the data that has informed them – ask for the data. In the case above, immaturity felt like a judgement; what was the data and also the consequences of the behaviour?
* People often don't have the lexicon to describe behavioural outcomes – keep asking for clarity. In the case above, what

outcomes were the organisation hoping for that were different from the ones they were getting currently (rather than what were the new behaviours)?

✳ Hold the sponsor to account and ensure specificity in what they say – dig deeper, stay curious, don't stick with their first answer.

✳ Send the sponsor questions/information ahead of time so they can prepare in advance and know what to expect (see below for an example).

✳ Be clear on your role as coach.

✳ Be clear on who/how the notes from the meeting will be captured.

✳ Be clear on how progress will be captured (and if/how that gets fed back).

This is what I (Clare) ask of line managers or sponsors when setting up a three-way conversation. Ideally, the coaching custodian should have this discussion with each sponsor, but this often slips between the cracks, so here's a belt and braces approach.

## ⬇ Communication to a sponsor to prepare them for the tripartite meeting

Coaching is exponentially more successful if you, the sponsor, are an integral partner in the process and give support and feedback on progress on a day-to-day basis. I'd ask that you:

» work with [name] to identify strengths, development areas and issues to be addressed before the coaching commences

» provide input on areas for goal setting for the coaching

» clarify expectations

» make the necessary resources available

» release the individual from their work to attend their coaching sessions on time

» encourage and celebrate wins

» provide feedback on progress (vs completion) on a regular basis

» respect the confidentiality of the coaching relationship.

To help everyone work towards the same outcome, it would be useful if you could consider the following questions before we meet. Ideally, the two of you should discuss these before we meet together so that this isn't a surprise to them.

» What's the reason for asking for coaching?

» What's a good outcome for the team? For the organisation? Any other stakeholders?

» If this coaching is successful, what will be different?

» What forces will work in support of the outcomes?

» What might get in the way?

» How have you contributed to where [name] is today? What have you done to help or hinder them?

» What's your strategy for ensuring that [name] gets the support they need going forward?

» What will you do to support [name] in these coaching outcomes?

» What can they count on you for?

» What's your commitment to them?

» Who else needs to offer support and how?

» How will you recognise positive change as it occurs?

» What return on investment do you need to see? How will you measure that (three months, six months and/ or nine months from now)?

» What are you already measuring?

» If these changes aren't possible, what will be the implications?

# Summary

As with every part of the thinker experience, the tripartite meeting sets up the coaching for agency. It's seen as good practice in the industry to make sure that the organisation gets what it wants from its investment. But it's not just about the organisation.

**The tripartite is equally about the needs and desires of the thinker, giving them agency to ask clarification questions, discuss obstacles that the line manager might be able to remove and ask for necessary resources.**

Of course, this isn't the last time that the two of them will talk, and as the coaching continues, the thinker will have ample opportunity to have more one-to-one conversations with their manager as they identify further systemic obstacles and resource needs.

## Reflective practice

* What do *you* believe about three-way contracting in relation to coaching readiness?
* Which of your values are showing up (or even being triggered) as you read this chapter? What does that tell you?
* What will you ask for and from whom? Which of these boundaries are non-negotiable and in which circumstances might you flex?
* What's the one thing you'll commit to experiment with that will make a marginal gain in the coaching readiness of the people with whom you work?

# Chapter 10

# Preparation through a coaching readiness lens

You've spoken to the thinker about the whole coaching experience at the contracting stage, including any preparation that they might do to wring the most value out of the time you have together. It's their choice as to whether they use any preparatory materials, but you can furnish the thinker with them and leave the choice to them. What's your process here? Do you ask them to complete any big-picture preparation at the outset of the coaching? Do you send them a preparation form before each session? How does each of your preparation sheets bring out their coaching readiness mindset?

In many ways, it doesn't matter what their answers are. Those answers are more important for the thinker to understand themselves than they are for the coach to understand them. **The questions are building their independent critical thinking muscles. They might not be easy to answer, but no one ever said that coaching would be easy!**

I have included example preparatory materials below, but please think these through for yourself as to what you want them to achieve, particularly from a coaching readiness perspective. Alongside the preparatory sheets, you may wish to remind thinkers about the optimal location for new thinking, for example, finding a private space. They can't think well if they believe they can be overheard. They also don't tend to think afresh when they're sitting in the chair where the issue originated in the first place (see Shift 72 in *The Transformational Coach*). Do they have a window that they can look out of to see the horizon and in doing so broaden their view? Might they wish to take their phone out for a walk if you work together virtually, so that they get oxygen to stimulate their brain and access to nature to restore their attention (Kaplan 1995)?

You may also wish to remind them to be well hydrated and fed, ideally with brain-friendly food (Mosconi 2019) rather than ultra-processed food (Van Tulleken 2023). This all sets them up for better thinking, as does sleep (Mosley 2023). With their agreement at the contracting stage, you might even send out a checklist before each session (see example below), reminding them of these good practices. Busyness may well get in the way, but if they've agreed to a nudge, a friendly encouragement (without being parental) wouldn't go amiss.

Then there's the way in which they clear their diary before and after a coaching session. I know from my own experience that people have a tough time transitioning from one meeting to another without a break in between to shift gears. If they skid straight from a meeting into coaching, there's often cognitive load left over. **Good endings enable us to make great beginnings, and that applies to meetings just as much as big change** (Bridges 2004).

You can encourage this in your contracting conversation and you might need to hold them to any agreement they make around this so that they have time to rehydrate, refuel or use the bathroom, not to mention closing down their thinking from the last meeting to allow space for new thinking in coaching.

## ⏻ Coaching joining instructions

As your coach, I will:

» support you by delivering focused, non-directive coaching, asking questions that tap into your wisdom and experience, in service of you

» challenge you to the degree that's useful to you and your progress

» remain completely focused on you in our coaching time

> » not tell you what to do or share my experiences with you, because I believe that only you can decide what's right for you, and that you can move forward on anything you bring to coaching
> » be completely non-judgemental and totally committed to your success
> » manage the structure and time of our sessions
> » remain alert to indications that there's a shift in the value received from the coaching relationship, and check in with you to understand how our partnership is working and where we might need to change
> » discuss with you how you might access counselling, therapy, your doctor, a legal or financial advisor or other professional practitioner, should coaching appear not to be right for you at any point in the coaching process.

I make no guarantee as to the results achieved, nor do I take responsibility for the results achieved from the coaching. Decisions and results are in your hands. You are responsible for your own achievements and success. I shall not be held accountable for any specific action you may or may not take to attain specific goals. I shall not be liable towards you or the sponsor for the result of actions taken by you in the course of this coaching programme.

## How the sessions work
*Before sessions:*

> » Diarise time out before each session so that you're hydrated and brain-fed and have taken care of other biological needs, ready to get the most value from the session right from the start. Get some fresh air and take a short walk to oxygenate your brain for thinking acuity.
> » Identify a coaching topic for every session related to

your overall coaching focus, whether that be an issue, an obstacle or an opportunity.

*In sessions:*

» Focus on new thinking rather than going over old ground so that you can get the most value from the session.

» Be fully present in our coaching sessions. Put your phone away and turn off messaging services on your laptop.

» Find a private space where you won't be interrupted or overheard so that you can speak candidly.

» Be honest with yourself and with me.

» Challenge your assumptions and explore your feelings and motivations in order to make longer-term changes rather than quick fixes.

» Stretch yourself and take risks; try new things; be prepared for discomfort.

» Take your own notes about what you're learning and to track your progress.

» Respect that coaching is non-directive and don't ask me to solve things for you.

» Share what you need from me, especially where you'd like us to agree a new way of working.

» Value and respect the time we have together by turning up on time every time.

*Between sessions:*

» Diarise time out after the session to reflect on your learning.

» Experiment and reflect in between sessions to move yourself forward, following through on your promises to yourself.

» Get the support you need to make change.

» Ask others for feedback about your progress.

» Respect the confidentiality of the relationship and understand the exceptions to confidentiality laid out in our contract.

(Adapted from Brenton Hague's coaching contract, with permission.)

## ⏻ Session preparation for the thinker

In order to get the most value out of each session we spend together, you may wish to spend time before each call thinking through what you want us to focus on.

**What I've learned since the last session:**
» What progress have I made since our last coaching session?
» What are my (micro-)moments of pride?
» What have I learned about myself as a result of that progress?
» How might I apply that learning in other areas of my life and work?

**What's the most important work I can bring to coaching in this session?**
» What do I and my stakeholders (boss, direct reports, customers, family, society, etc) need me to address in this session?
» What's the relationship between these issues and my overall coaching goals (and/or are my coaching goals shifting)?
» What thinking have I already done around this?

**My attitudes and motivation towards the coaching conversation and coaching relationship:**
» What's important to me about this at this moment in time?

» How prepared am I to think deeply about this, no matter where it might take me?

» What's in my control with regard to resolving this?

**Thinking accelerators:**

How would I rate myself on a scale of 1–5 on the following right now, with 5 being 'I'm completely in alignment'?

» I get enough sleep to enable me to think clearly.

» The level of my physical activity promotes my mental acuity.

» I take myself to a green space at least once a day to restore my attention (whether a forest, a park, a common, a scrap of land at the end of my street).

» My diet supports critical thinking.

» I drink enough water to keep my brain hydrated and at peak thinking capacity.

» I proactively keep my stress levels under control.

» I'm purposeful in my use of technology so as not to drain my energy.

How might I move the dial on these thinking accelerators to support my thinking in and out of the coaching sessions?

**Preparatory logistics for this coaching session:**

» I've blocked time before the coaching session to prepare mentally.

» I've blocked time before the coaching session to prepare my body (rehydrating, feeding my brain and using the bathroom).

» I've blocked time after the coaching session to reflect.

» I commit to turning up on time, every time.

» I commit to switching off distractions for the duration of the coaching session.

» I commit to carving out deep thinking time in my diary, over and above my coaching.

# Summary

Everything you do and say throughout the coaching experience is an opportunity to build coaching readiness, including any 'joining instructions' you design and any session preparation you decide to send. To build agency, I encourage you to think about the wording. What will benefit the people with whom you work?

## Reflective practice

✳ What do *you* believe about preparatory reflection for the thinker in relation to coaching readiness?

✳ Which of your values are showing up (or even being triggered) as you read this chapter? What does that tell you?

✳ What will you ask for and from whom? Which of these boundaries are non-negotiable and in which circumstances might you flex?

✳ What's the one thing you'll commit to experiment with that will make a marginal gain in the coaching readiness of the people with whom you work?

# Chapter 11

# Session by session through a coachability lens

You've made it through the set-up phase of the coaching experience, which is a much more important phase in terms of screening for and enhancing coaching readiness than you might historically have given it credit for; now you're ready to partner with the thinker session by session to draw out their coachability. You'll notice that shift here from my use of coaching readiness to coachability. That is on purpose as it's no longer about screening for and preparing their readiness, but rather enhancing their innate coachability.

Session (small c) contracting has been covered in Chapter 8. Now the focus turns to other aspects of enhancing the thinker's agency.

Bear in mind that I see our role as coaches to be non-directive and person centred and this informs how I go about developing agency. As Robert Biswas-Diener writes (2023), 'Coaching... is not about clients achieving their goals. That's the client's business. My business is engaging them in a process of self-directed learning.' As you embark on considering agency, session by session, be informed by this mindset and the research that backs it up about non-directive coaching leading to more creative insights than directive coaching or self-rumination (Bartolome et al 2022). Please don't steal the thinker's learning (Anagnostakis 2023).

**Relationship habits 'set like cement'** (Gottlieb 2024). So, start as you mean to go on. If you get hooked into giving advice at the start of the relationship, they'll continue to expect that and it will be hard to wean them off it. If you start by relaying the question back to them to find their own answers, they'll be building that muscle from day one. Interrupt (Shift 4 in *The Transformational Coach*) in service of coachability from the beginning, too – or insert any intuitions you sense. The same goes for all of your relationship habits with the thinker.

Social psychologist Harry T Reis (2007) has found that **relationships are stronger when we perceive that the other person is responsive to us**.

Responsiveness means:

✳ Understanding: my coach knows how I see myself and what's important to me.
✳ Validation: my coach respects who I am and what I want.
✳ Caring: my coach takes active and supportive steps in helping me to meet my needs (though, in coaching, you're not doing anything for them that they could do for themselves).

How can you show understanding, validation and caring to build a better relationship and in turn build their own understanding, validation and caring for themselves? **Together, you're aiming for agency and self-authorship.**

*The Transformational Coach* gives you many ways in which to access that agency, encouraging the thinker to think for themselves, so please treat that book as a companion to this chapter in particular. Here, I'll endeavour to introduce new content that I didn't cover in that book.

# Developing curiosity, growth mindset and hope

Is curiosity something you can cultivate? I believe it is. Carol Dweck (2017) sees it as possible too, in her work on 'growth mindset'. This mindset underpins learning. Coaching is about learning – not through teaching but via thinking.

If a thinker comes to coaching believing that there's only one right answer (a fixed mindset, ostensibly developed to pass exams), the coaching may feel more difficult for them. As coaches, we can nurture more of the growth mindset, the desire to find multiple ways of seeing the world, by adopting a few underpinning mindsets of our own. First, that **coaching is 'a joint endeavour to discover new thinking'** (Norman 2022). *New* thinking, not *known* thinking (see Shift 4 in *The Transformational Coach*).

This person you're working with is unique, as is their context, their personality, their stakeholders, their lived experience – I could go on. Because of this, the coach's known thinking about what has worked for others in the past won't be a perfect fit for this incomparable individual. This moment in time isn't the same as any other moment you've faced before in coaching or, as the Japanese would say, *'ichi-go, ichi-e'*, which means that this moment in time has never happened before and will never happen ever again – it's a one-off. It's a good reminder for coaches (me included) that you must meet the thinker where *they* are and enable them to be curious about their distinctive situation to get to brand-new thinking that's relevant for them in their unique situation.

Yes, I know, other people have encountered similar things in the past, and yes, normalising what they're encountering can be useful, but providing a one-size-fits-all answer isn't useful. Indeed, that undermines curiosity and learning – and agency to find a personal fit.

Second, creating value is important in coaching, but your role as coach is to cultivate that value via the thinker rather than taking that mantle for yourself. Yes, the coach has the thinker's best interests at heart, but **that best interest is in building their thinking muscles rather than doing the thinking for them**. (See the summary in *The Transformational Coach*.)

Third, as you know, the thinker is 'creative, resourceful and whole' and therefore they're perfectly capable of creating that value (see Shift 58 in *The Transformational Coach*). By seeing the thinker as creative, resourceful and whole, you're also holding in mind the best version of this person in front of you that they might have forgotten about (Eisenstein 2018). Sometimes the thinker has lost their own connection with this best self and you can rekindle hope by reconnecting them with the wholeness of who they are.

Tapping into their own resourcefulness involves (among other things) cultivating hope within the thinker, hope that they can go forward once coaching has finished: '...hopeful thought reflects the belief that one can find pathways to desired goals and become motivated to use those pathways' (Snyder et al 2021).

According to McKenna and Davis (2009), **15 per cent of the effectiveness of therapy [coaching] can be attributed to the active ingredient of expectancy and hope as a placebo.**

The research by Snyder et al suggests the following as hope building:

* recognising the 'possibilities of intermediate goal attainment'
* a belief in the 'capabilities at generating workable routes to desired goals'
* developing agency thinking such as 'I can do this' and 'I'm not going to be stopped'
* drawing on the emotion of past positive experiences of pathway thinking (finding a workable route towards goal achievement) and agency thinking (a belief that you can overcome barriers along the path to a goal).

There are many other tools at our disposal for creating hope, such as reframing, evidence-based questioning, shifting from a scarcity mentality to an abundance mentality (Covey 1999), gratitude, celebrating the small wins and recognising progress towards goals, visualisation of a different future, building and leveraging social support, having even the smallest of epiphanies/ new ways of seeing things, and creating moments of pride (Heath and Heath 2017). These are all well within the coach's capabilities to bring to the coaching table.

Fourth, the coach invites the thinker into what Berne would call the Adult ego state. That means being in Adult yourself, rather than Parent inviting the thinker into Child. **Don't infantilise them.** (See Shift 39 in *The Transformational Coach*.)

And fifth, relationship is key; but that doesn't mean support, support, support without challenge. **They're not paying for a cosy chat. Lean into challenge** (see Shifts 5 and 29 in *The Transformational Coach*).

# Challenge through feedback

One such challenge is underpinned by a belief that **who they are in coaching is (likely) how they are in life and work.** You might say that about yourself as a coach: 'Who I am is how I coach.' 'Who they are in coaching is how they are in life and work' is a mirror image of that and can be useful for giving the thinker feedback about how you experience them in coaching and what you notice as an impact on yourself, and whether the thinker perceives that to be how they might be experienced by others in their work and home life. This can include positive experiences of the thinker or disconcerting experiences, all offered from an Adult to Adult ego state, not Parent to Child, and with no attachment to their consideration of the feedback.

For example, you might give them feedback about how their low mood has an impact on you, or how their avoidance of decision making or going round in circles has an impact on you, and then ask a question about how these might be perceived by the people they encounter on a daily basis. Of course, this is a space where you want them to feel safe to be themselves *and* this is all data for them to consider. This is particularly pertinent when they're working on something specific through coaching and demonstrating contraindications to that in the coaching.

> ⭐ For example, I've coached people who've been working on becoming more succinct in their communication with their peers and boss. If I were to accede to long, detailed stories in coaching, I'd be colluding with this behaviour, which is the opposite of what the thinker said they wanted. But if I challenge them to treat this coaching as a learning laboratory, it gives them a chance to experiment in order to carry those experiments back into their usual working world. Your role is to support them to make sustainable changes and you can do that by holding up a mirror when you experience behaviours that are contrary to their intended aims.

# Learning to think

While the coach supports and challenges the thinkers with whom they work to move towards the changes they desire, you're concurrently supporting them to build their own thinking muscles – learning how to be self-directed learners. This will serve them well in between sessions and after the coaching assignment is complete.

By its very nature, coaching gives the thinker time to think, and you can extend the silences longer than you might be comfortable with to continue to allow them to think for themselves rather than stepping in to rescue them from live silence (see Shift 34 in *The Transformational Coach*).

Also partner with the thinker by inviting them to respond in any way to your contributions and accept their response (PCC Marker 4.4 in the ICF Competencies – see Bibliography). **Coaching is often about the thinker learning to stand up for their needs, and doing so with you is a safe practice ground.**

My former colleague at Accenture, Dana Koch (2024), has discovered a set of durable learning principles that underpin self-directed learning, and you can use these to inform the shape of your coaching. He sees self-directed learning as essential to survival within the working world, which is changing so rapidly. Employees can no longer expect the hand holding of days gone by, where there was ample time for the learning and development function to design and deliver training on the change heading towards their organisational world. Employees need to be proactive in their pursuit of learning to keep up with, if not stay ahead of, change.

What are these durable learning principles and how can you incorporate them into the way you coach, so that the thinker builds their own thinking muscles?

1. Learning is relevant. It's of the moment, addressing current needs. This is already true of coaching as you work with the thinker where they are in the moment, not where they

were in the last session (see Shift 73 in *The Transformational Coach).* Relevance is about working with the right person on their real-world goals, at the right time, reminding you of the importance of checking that coaching is a good fit for the person before you agree to begin to work together – and to continue checking in about the relevance of the goals they set at the start of the coaching, which may well have developed or changed completely.

2. Learning is contextual in that it connects to existing knowledge and mental models. As coach, you support the thinker to *build* on what they already know (rather than going over that old ground) and enable them to see the bigger picture with questions about the system.

3. Learning is engaging. You've discovered how coaching can build hope (page 126) as a means to engage and motivate. It's dynamic in that the thinker is encouraged to think actively rather than consuming content passively. It keeps their attention by focusing on their progress throughout a session. For example, 'What do you know now that you didn't know before?' or 'You said you wanted x today – what progress have you made towards that?' (see Shift 3 in *The Transformational Coach*).

   Your coaching will ideally use a variety of modalities, accessing multiple intelligences (see Shift 42). This will engage all parts of the thinker, not just their cerebral knowing.

   In order to be fully engaging, the thinker needs to be free of distractions so that they can avoid task switching (for example, when a message pops up on their laptop in the middle of a virtual coaching session), which reduces their ability to think.

   According to Koch's research, humans have a 20-minute neurological limit on attention, suggesting that shorter sessions will engage them better and/or that you should pause every 20 minutes to ask where they are now and where they want to go next in their thinking. The optimal amount of time for a coaching programme? 'If the coaching offer is shorter – perhaps limited to four or six sessions – clients will make an effort to still take away a lot' (De Haan 2023).

4. Learning is effortful. Hard thinking is good for creating a sense of agency. It's an emotional investment, not just showing up. Think of coaching as 'cognitive callisthenics where [the thinker] experiences brain sweat and comes out stronger' (Koch 2024). Facing seemingly insurmountable challenges enables the thinker to grow more than backing off from those challenges or somehow making them easier. And the trial and error of experimentation in between coaching is to be encouraged, not avoided.

5. Learning is generative in that the learner constructs and articulates meaning, both in the session and between sessions. The coach encourages the thinker to elaborate in their own words rather than putting words into their mouth. Coaching enables the thinker to expand their mental models through questioning their own assumptions and paradigms. You might even invite the thinker to create meaningful learning artefacts, such as a photograph of a constellation they created that opened up new perspectives as reminders of what they're learning.

6. Learning is social, which means it happens in collaboration with others. That's the very crux of coaching, whether one-to-one or in a group or team.

7. Learning involves spaced practice. There's some recent research into the optimal spacing of coaching sessions. Erik De Haan has found that 'the more frequent the sessions, the higher the effectiveness' (2023) but they're still spaced. I might replace the word practice with experimentation, which I encourage in between coaching sessions. Variety of practice is also important, also including variety in the time of day and the location of coaching.

8. Learning is reflective. Reflection is about what has gone before (retrieval) and what's to come (generation). What has the thinker learned in the past that they can apply in this situation they're facing today? How might they tackle an upcoming opportunity?

Underlying these learning principles are learning accelerators (Koch 2024), or what I like to call thinking accelerators: sleep, exercise, attention restoration, nutrition, reduced stress. This is why it's in the thinker's interest for you to ask them to consider their sleep hygiene, exercise routines, time in nature, food intake and stress levels (as I do in the pre-coaching questionnaire that I send out, see the Appendix). I know I've repeated this message multiple times throughout the book, but these thinking accelerators feel important and are often overlooked.

What do you make of this? How might you incorporate these durable learning principles and thinking accelerators into your practice, if you haven't already?

# Progress through the sessions

As outlined in Chapter 3, when Sam and I introduced screening for coaching readiness, people move through stages of change (Prochaska et al 1994).

How might you, the coach, work with thinkers at each stage?

| Stage | What you might hear | How the coach might work with a thinker at this stage |
|---|---|---|
| Pre-con-templa-tion | 'I don't think I have a problem' | • This is most likely to happen in the pre-coaching stage. If the prospective thinker doesn't see an issue, it will be difficult to entice them into a curious mindset of change. You'll notice that there's more of a flavour of offering data and information here, which can still be done in a coach-like manner, but is a little more directive than you might like to be later on, once a person has wholeheartedly opted in to coaching.<br>• Use data to raise awareness of the impact and implications of how the thinker is, for example, prioritising, or whatever the developmental goal is (360° feedback, performance reports, tripartite input, psychometric). Personally, I'd ask a different coach to conduct 360°s and psychometrics (see Shift 78 in *The Transformational Coach* for my reasons, which map to agency).<br>• Offer, without attachment or parenting, examples of the impact of not changing.<br>• Encourage the thinker to become aware that they have choices, options and alternatives so they can calibrate their approach/behaviour if they choose to.<br>• Invite the thinker to identify different approaches to [prioritising] and/or signpost them toward alternative ideas. This isn't a call to action; it's about providing more data for the thinker to consider. |

| Contem-plation | 'I want to stop feeling so stuck' | • Partner co-creatively about how the thinker can make an emotional connection with the change and find the thing that will get and keep them motivated. For example, invite the thinker to write a letter as their ten-years-older self about how their future is different due to the changes they've made now. Or ask the thinker to identify a piece of music that could be their theme tune for this particular change.<br>• Keep checking in on their emotional connection to their goal: is it fit for purpose; has it changed?<br>• Build hope, as described on page 126.<br>• Invite the thinker to look for possibilities rather than certainties: good timing for change rather than perfect timing.<br>• Work with the realities of the situation rather than wishful thinking, yet look for the glimmers of hope. |
|---|---|---|
| Prepa-ration | 'I'm going to change' | • Invite the thinker to chunk down experiments to smaller achievable ones.<br>• Invite them to give themselves a deadline.<br>• Invite them to think about how they can secure support for change and from whom. |
| Action | 'I'm confi-dent I can make this happen' | • Invite the thinker to write down goals and objectives, as this increases the chances of successful achievement (Locke & Latham 2012).<br>• Acknowledge who they're being (for example, effortful, curious, deep thinking, a learner, an experimenter, anything that encourages them to continue to be a self-directed learner after the coaching is complete).<br>• Celebrate progress and milestones on the path towards the final goal (Amabile & Kramer 2011).<br>• Support the thinker in identifying rewards for achievement/progress.<br>• Find ways to keep the thinker positive.<br>• Encourage the thinker to elicit feedback and support from their support team. |

| Mainte-nance | 'I failed' | • Encourage the thinker to re-contract with their support group – giving them permission to feedback when/if they see something that's taking the thinker off track.<br>• Continue to recognise small wins to build self-belief and momentum (Amabile & Kramer 2011).<br>• Co-create a 'recovery plan' for the times when they fall off the wagon.<br>• Rehearse alternative scenarios together in preparation for conversations or presentations, for example.<br>• Encourage the application of some positive psychology – for example, a gratitude diary, random acts of kindness. |
|---|---|---|

*Table co-created with Sam Humphrey, adapted for coaching from the original work of Prochaska et al.*

# Difficult behaviours, not difficult thinkers

Julia Menaul has recorded a number of videos (see Bibliography) about difficult behaviours that you may encounter in coaching sessions. She suggests that the coach should treat them as difficult *behaviours*, not a difficult person. The thinker is behaving in ways that help them to cope.

You can bring the behaviour to their attention (see page 127 about feedback) and may need to do this multiple times, discussing alternative behaviours and new positive habits if they wish to, then reinforcing and celebrating any changes they make.

Julia identifies three behaviours that can feel hard for the coach to work with, perhaps even hinting at diminishing coachability. These are by no means the only behaviours you'll come across:

✳ disengagement
✳ defensiveness
✳ over-talkativeness.

Taking each in turn, how might you encounter them and what might you do to support the thinker to access their agency?

**The disengaged thinker:** This may show up as uninterested, sparse responses with little depth of thinking, little animation, not taking action, arriving late to sessions or cancelling at the last minute.

Given cultural differences, don't jump to conclusions about what this difference in self-expression is all about. Talk it through with them. Ask them what their energy levels or short responses mean for them.

Revisit whether this is the right time for them, whether they really want to make changes or have the capacity to make changes. Maybe there's some major stress or distress in their life that they hadn't accounted for when you first started working together, which may be taking their attention away from coaching.

Use Prochaska's model (see page 54) to decide together where they are in relation to readiness to change and whether they're ready for the work involved. Revisit their expectations around their own agency and self-efficacy to make change a reality.

You may feel as though you're working harder than them. Stop! This is their life, and the value that they get out of the sessions is commensurate with what they're willing to put in – not what you put in.

**The defensive thinker:** This may sound like blaming others, being seemingly negative, argumentative, resistant, dogmatic, entrenched, rationalising, making excuses.

There are all sorts of reasons that could be behind these behaviours, but you shouldn't try to interpret those reasons without asking them for the meaning that they're making. You can offer support and compassion and, with their permission, challenge their ways of being. What responsibility do they take for things not working out? How does that make them feel? What choices do they have? What agency do they have?

If they don't perceive defensiveness, you could invite them to watch a video of the coaching session and ask them what they notice. Do they wish to make changes? Where are they in Prochaska's model? Is this the right time for them to be in a coaching relationship?

**The talkative thinker:** This person may be sharing lots of context and background. They already know this story, but perhaps think that you need to know it too, in order to help them. Coaching is new territory for them and perhaps they don't (yet) comprehend that it's about getting to new thinking rather than going over old ground. It's possible that this is a mechanism to veer away from thinking more deeply, to avoid going to perceived scary new places, though you can't know this unless you ask. The danger is that you wait for them to finish... by which time, they've used half of the session to tell you things that they already know. This isn't creating value for them. You might think that new insights will emerge eventually, but often it's more detail of the story rather than a better understanding of themselves and the root causes of their situation.

Summarising what they say only leads to more story. So, you need to have the courage to interrupt known thinking in service of new thinking (see Shift 4 in *The Transformational Coach*) and to invite them to access new thinking via intelligences other than the overused cerebral, logical intelligence (see Shift 72).

# Cognitive distortion

It's normal for humans to distort the truth and fall into thinking traps.

For example, life experiences may have led the thinker to be predisposed to:

❋ catastrophising – seeing something bigger and worse than it really is
❋ all-or-nothing thinking – seeing things as black or white,

extreme thinking, either/or, one end of a spectrum or the other
* overgeneralisation – drawing broad conclusions from isolated incidents
* focusing only on negative feedback – discounting the positives.

These are ways of thinking that can keep the thinker knowingly or more likely unconsciously trapped in unhelpful patterns. They hint at a dearth of agency, which is why it's important for us to look at them in relation to coachability.

As coaches, we can be on the lookout for these all-too-common distortions, to enable the thinker to reclaim their agency.

See if you recognise yourself and/or the thinkers with whom you work in any of the following:

| Thinking trap | Description | Example replacement thought |
|---|---|---|
| **All-or-nothing thinking** | Seeing everything as black or white, for example, 'I lost my job. I'm a complete failure at everything.' 'This was a complete waste of time. I learned nothing from it.' | 'Life is full of imperfect situations. I can learn from this.' What's the third (and fourth and fifth) alternative to this either/or thinking? |
| **Mind-reading** | Jumping to the conclusion that someone's thinking the worst about you, even though you have no evidence of that, for example, 'They never phone me, so they must not really care about me.' | 'I can't read minds. If I want to know what someone's thinking, I can ask.' |
| **Fortune telling** | Predicting what will happen ahead of time, such as 'I'm going to fail this exam today.' | 'I can't predict the future. I may have some hunches, but they're not necessarily going to come true. |

(continued overleaf)

| Labelling | Labelling yourself or others as, for example, lazy or stupid or a failure (often after just one event). | 'There's no need to judge myself or others.' 'How might I show compassion to myself and/or others?' 'I am/they are human.' |
|---|---|---|
| Emotional reasoning | Believing something to be true as a result of the emotion you feel, for example, 'I feel useless, therefore I'm useless.' | 'My feelings offer me insights, but they are not necessarily evidence of reality.' |
| Shoulds/ shouldn'ts Musts/ mustn'ts | Often come from what you believe others think you should or shouldn't do or be; a sense of obligation, often accompanied by guilt. | 'I can decide for myself what I wish to do or not do/ be or not be.' |
| Personalisation | Taking responsibility for something that's not necessarily yours to feel responsible for, such as a leader blaming themselves for something out of their control. | 'No one is to blame here.' The system may need to be adjusted to rectify the issue at a macro level. |
| Blaming | Putting all the responsibility on someone else, when you contribute in some way too. | 'What's my part of the problem here? And what's theirs?' |
| Catastrophising | Assuming the worst possible outcome or feeling the worst possible feeling when something's uncomfortable. | 'It is what it is/will be what it will be, no more and no less.' |
| Overgeneralisation | Often includes words such as never, always, every – for example, 'This always happens to me.' | 'It's entirely possible that something different will happen next time.' |
| Minimising | Making oneself or one's achievements insignificant by minimising them, for example, 'It was nothing,' | 'I can honour my strengths and achievements and not take away from anyone else's strengths and achievements.' |

*Based on the work of Ellis (1957) and Beck (1972).*

How might you help yourself and the thinkers with whom you work to embrace the replacement thoughts? Perhaps by asking them what the evidence is and the counterevidence and therefore whether and how they might wish to reframe their thinking to be more useful.

# Limiting beliefs

At first glance, limiting beliefs might suggest a dearth of coachability – at least, perhaps, in the historical definition of coachability. But you'll have encountered limiting beliefs many, many times in coaching and they require empathy and challenge in equal measure.

How many times have you heard yourself or the thinkers with whom you work say words to the effect of:

* I can't.
* I'm not good enough.
* They're better than me.
* I don't have enough experience.
* I'm not clever enough.
* I'm too old.
* I won't be the best, so what's the point in applying?
* I don't have the funds.
* I'm going to fail.

These limiting beliefs and many others show signs of fear and a desire to protect oneself, and there's an inherent lack of agency and self-efficacy within them. They may be borne out of fear of the unknown, memories of past experiences or an imposter phenomenon ('I'll be found out as a fraud, above my station', Clance & Imes 1978). **You can support the thinker to rediscover their agency by working at the level of belief.**

If the limiting belief is still lurking in the background, it's rarely enough to gloss over the beliefs with positive mantras. Instead, ask the thinker these questions (adapted from Gil Schwenk's unpublished reframing beliefs model, in turn adapted from neuro-linguistic programming (NLP) and Tony Robbins):

✳ What is your belief?
✳ Where does this belief come from (parental, school, peer, workplace or other external influences)?
✳ What concrete, factual evidence do you have to support that belief?
✳ What assumptions are you making that come from your imagination and perceptions?
✳ What assumptions are you making based on others' say-so?
✳ What have been the benefits to you of holding this belief/ thought?
✳ What have been the costs to you in holding this belief/ thought?

And then this second set of questions:

✳ What's your new belief that you now choose to believe? Write it using positive language in the present tense.
✳ Why do you choose to believe that?
✳ What are the benefits to you of choosing this belief?
✳ What are the costs to you of choosing this belief?
✳ What evidence do you already have to support your new belief?
✳ Now say, 'I give myself permission to believe....'
✳ Repeat as often as possible to reinforce it and replace the old belief.

## Possibility

*The Art of Possibility* (Zander & Zander 2000) is one of my favourite books, as much for the title as for the content. Coaching is all about possibilities and looking for new ways of doing and being, even when some of these might be mere glimmers of hope. But in order to find those new ways of doing and being, you need to believe in the art of the possible.

I'm not a Pollyanna by any stretch of the imagination, but I am more of a glass-half-full kind of person than a glass-half-empty one.

I'm (generally) hopeful that things can and will work out.

I'm hopeful that I can and will find ways forward, even when I currently feel stuck.

I'm hopeful that there will be a multitude of possibilities and options that I hadn't even imagined before I speak with a coach about whatever the blockage is.

You and/or the thinkers with whom you work might be more pessimistic than me – or you/they might call that realism. But encourage the thinker to come to coaching with an open mind that new ideas are lurking underneath the surface, or perhaps by digging a bit deeper. If the insights were obvious, the thinker wouldn't need a coach – but just because those new ideas are not obvious to them before the coaching conversation doesn't mean the insights won't become obvious.

In fact, many people leave a coaching conversation saying, 'That seems so obvious now that I say it out loud. Why couldn't I have thought about that on my own?'

Please believe that the thinkers with whom you work will find the obvious – and less than obvious – answers to their conundrums by talking them through. That belief will really help them to make headway, much more than being pessimistic or defeatist.

And here's a question that I love as an optimist: **'What would be the best possible outcome from this coaching?'**

Not an average outcome, but the best possible. Let's aim for great, not good. Let's believe that thinkers can get further than they think they can – both in the coaching programme and in each coaching session.

When asked what they want from a coaching session, some thinkers say that what they want might be a little too ambitious for the time you have together and they come back from that point to something smaller. But let's partner with the thinker to be ambitious and see what might be possible.

# Summary

When it comes to building their thinking muscles session by session, there are some people for whom you'll need a very light touch. Personally, I love working with people who are self-propelled and willing to go to the sometimes difficult places to figure things out for themselves.

Sometimes, people (the same ones or different) might need a few more nudges to access their innermost thoughts, feelings and senses. That's normal, especially where they're not so used to thinking for themselves.

Your role as coach is to check out and arrest with the thinker any embryonic declines in coachability, and to enable the thinker to go from good to better in their processing, whatever that means for them.

## Reflective practice

* What do *you* believe about your role in coaching sessions in relation to enhancing coachability and agency?
* Which of your values are showing up (or even being triggered) as you read this chapter? What does that tell you?
* What will you ask for and from whom? Which of these boundaries are non-negotiable and in which circumstances might you flex?
* What's the one thing you'll commit to experiment with that will make a marginal gain in the coachability and agency of the people with whom you work?

# Chapter 12

# Post-session integration through a coachability lens

As with every part of the thinker experience, it's important to use the opportunity for post-session reflection as another element of incrementally building agency and coachability.

There are two parts to this post-session integration:

1. setting up the thinker for success at the end of the coaching session itself
2. post-session reflective practice for the thinker.

## Closing the session with agency in mind

The end of a coaching session is just as important as the beginning. It needs ample time to wrap the learning up well, such that the thinker reminds themselves about the application in between sessions of the new thinking they've had. As I wrote in *The Transformational Coach* (Shift 61), the (real) work happens when the thinker and coach are apart.

**Closing the session fully allows for continued new thinking afterwards** (Shift 79) and it creates even more agency and a desire in the thinker to create value.

These are the kinds of questions I generally use to close a session with agency in mind, using the acronym C-L-O-S-E.

# ↻ Closing a coaching session

| Consolida-tion | • We have x minutes left. You said you wanted y today. What progress have you made towards that?<br>• How will you continue to add value for yourself between now and the next time we meet?<br>• What experiments are you committing to after the session that will continue your progress? [Or] What enquiry are you taking away with you today? |
|---|---|
| Learning | • What are you hoping to learn or gain from your experiments?<br>• What have you learned about yourself today that you can apply in this situation and beyond? |
| Obstacles | • What might stop you? [Or] What might trip you up?<br>• What part of you is resisting what you're saying to yourself right now? |
| Support | • What support mechanisms might you put in place?<br>• What external resources can you draw on?<br>• Which of your strengths will you draw on to support you?<br>• I'd like to celebrate your progress today and appreciate your [insert what you appreciate about them as a person].<br>• What beliefs are you crafting that could sustain you? |
| End | • What final words of wisdom would you like to give yourself as we draw to a close?<br>• On that note, is that a good place to end? |

Notice that I don't offer to hold them accountable, but rather I ask them who in their day-to-day life they could ask to support them. And more importantly, what strengths of their own can they draw on. This serves them better in the long run when coach and thinker are no longer working together.

You may have additional ways of creating that agency and you may have got into some habits that undermine the thinker's agency. Take a moment to reflect on how you could beef up this part of your coaching for the benefit of the thinker's agency.

# Post-session reflective practice

Just as it can be useful to thinkers to have a structure for their preparation for coaching, it can be equally useful to have a set of reflective questions that capture the learning after the session. This is to enable the thinker, not the coach, to keep track of their progress and go deeper in their thinking. Tracking their own progress is part of taking accountability, which in turn creates more self-efficacy and agency. Deepening their thinking is also a requisite for self-efficacy and agency – all in the name of coachability.

**Any progress is good progress, because a feeling of progress gives the thinker momentum to continue** (Amabile & Kramer 2011), but they have to recognise that progress to fuel the motivation to continue. Together, you can reflect on progress in the session and encourage it after the session too.

Below you can find examples of post-session reflection questions that support this feeling of progress and deepen the learning, connecting back to the original goals for the coaching. Make it your own, based on your beliefs about how progress, learning and goals support the coaching readiness of the thinker – their sense of agency, self-efficacy and building independent critical thinking.

They may wish to do this reflection immediately after the coaching while it's fresh; or they may choose to come back to it once the dust has settled. Reflectors in particular might want to ponder for a few days before they come back to this. That said, encouraging a 15-minute block of non-meeting time after the coaching session can help the thinker build good habits around energy management and thinking management, allowing them to enter their next meeting rehydrated, refuelled and refreshed.

One of the questions you may have asked at the end of the coaching session might be about the support they can draw on at work and/or at home to help them with the research, thinking, reflection or action that they chose to commit to in between sessions. This 15-minute window can also be a good time to set up time with those people or ask them directly – striking while the iron is hot. Peer support is really important in helping to remove a person's sense of isolation in tackling issues that might otherwise feel difficult to resolve alone. After all, the coach isn't with them all of the time. Supporting the thinker to find accountability buddies and/or a 'board of personal directors' who offer different things to the thinker (a sounding board, mentoring, feedback, brainstorming, etc) sets them up for success when the coaching has finished.

## ↻ Post-session reflection for the thinker

The purpose of this reflection document is to enable you to capture your learning and actions from the coaching session. It's entirely up to you whether and when you use this to keep track of your progress.

**Learning:**
»   What new ideas and insights have I gained?
»   What do I need to think about more deeply?

**Intention:**
»   How am I going to put this learning into practice?
»   What do I want to explore with other people?
»   How will I show up differently each day as the person I want to become?

**Process:**
»   Was I sufficiently open and honest with myself?
»   What could I have done to extract more value from the conversation?
»   What will I do differently in preparing for the next coaching session?

*Adapted from David Clutterbuck's 4i's model  – issues, ideas, insights, intentions (2022).*

146

# Summary

Hopefully, it has registered by now that every part of the coaching experience is an opportunity to enhance coachability and agency, including post-session integration. The work happens when you and the thinker are apart (Shift 61 in *The Transformational Coach*), just as much as, if not more than, when you're together. You can encourage agency to build in between coaching sessions through experiments and progress of whatever kind, even when you're not together. This is their work, not yours.

## Reflective practice

❋ What do *you* believe about post-session integration in relation to agency?

❋ Which of your values are showing up (or even being triggered) as you read this chapter? What does that tell you?

❋ What will you ask for and from whom? Which of these boundaries are non-negotiable and in which circumstances might you flex?

❋ What's the one thing you'll commit to experiment with that will make a marginal gain in the agency of the people with whom you work?

# Chapter 13

# Re-contracting through a coachability lens

As you work your way through the coaching experience, you'll frequently re-contract. My focus in this book is to look at it through the lens of coachability and agency.

I've already alluded to having a conversation with the thinker whenever you spot signs of defensiveness, disengagement, limiting beliefs, thinking traps and other ways in which they might be giving away their power and agency. You can do this in the moment. Assuming these conversations enable you to agree to continue working together, you'll still wish to re-contract at the halfway point of your coaching, to be sure that you're both working well together.

Start with reflections on their progress, particularly in relation to what they wanted from coaching and what they're learning about themselves:

'You said you wanted [outcome] from coaching. What progress have you made towards that so far?'

'What have you learned about yourself as a result of the experiments that you've been testing out?'

'Given all of that, what's our focus for the remaining x sessions of coaching?'

Then move on to how you can each contribute to their momentum going forward. **This is as much about how they're showing up as it is about how you're showing up.** So, don't be tempted to only ask a question akin to 'How am I doing as your coach?' This is a partnership, after all.

The better question is something along the lines of:

'How are we working together so far?' or 'How are you expe-riencing the space between us today?'

Or perhaps, 'How might we challenge ourselves in the way we work together so that you can create optimal value for yourself?'

You may wish to unpack that a little more, for example:

'Imagine a half hour from now, as you look back at the session. What will be unspoken between us in the way we are working?'

'What might you personally stop/start/continue to get the most value from this coaching?'

And then:

'What might I stop/start/continue to support and challenge you to step further into your agency in this change journey?'

If it feels as if they're giving away their autonomy by asking for more mentoring than coaching, this is a good place to reconsider together what coaching is and how coaching can support them to build their own thinking muscles and create self-efficacy.

If you find yourself as coach being hooked into taking more responsibility, you're likely to further diminish the thinker's agency. Consider where this might be coming from in the system rather than the individual. Are you filling a gap that the line manager should by rights be filling? Is the boss not very nurturing, so you play that role instead? Is the thinker in danger of losing their job, so you feel more responsibility to rescue? Supervision can support you in figuring out what in the system is hooking you into further limiting the thinker's agency. And a re-contracting conversation is key to decide together how to work with that.

You may re-contract for other things at this point too, such as location, session duration or session spacing, all of which might have some bearing on their agency or at least give them the chance to renegotiate using their growing sense of agency to ask for what they need.

# Summary

Re-contracting is another opportunity for agency building. It gives the thinker a chance to ask for what they need and negotiate with you for any changes that the two of you wish to make. This is practice ground for them, a safe place to assert their needs such that they build that muscle. It's also a space for you to challenge them to step into their own self-efficacy even more.

## Reflective practice

* What do *you* believe about re-contracting in relation to agency?
* Which of your values are showing up (or even being triggered) as you read this chapter? What does that tell you?
* What will you ask for and from whom? Which of these boundaries are non-negotiable and in which circumstances might you flex?
* What's the one thing you'll commit to experiment with that will make a marginal gain in the agency of the people with whom you work?

# Chapter 14

## Closing through a coachability lens

All good things must come to an end – including coaching. This is yet another opportunity to co-create coachability, agency and self-efficacy in the thinker. Given everything you've digested so far, the thinker should by now be feeling ready for independent thinking without their coach. That's your role, to do yourself out of a job. And you can support them at this point in the coaching experience to think through this ending and the new chapter that they're entering into.

According to William Bridges (2004), good endings require several things in order to make a great new beginning:

＊ Deconstruct the old – in this case, reviewing the coaching and working out how you wish to co-create the ending.
＊ Recognise any losses – in this case, the loss of this working relationship, possibly the loss of being in contact from here on.
＊ Celebrate the ending – in whatever way feels appropriate to you both (that might be a shared cake, the gift of a book that matches their ongoing learning, a card that they write to themselves to be sent back to them in six months' time, etc).

You can help thinkers to work through these by asking them to reflect on these questions below before or during the last coaching session (adapted from unpublished work by Diane Clutterbuck and William Bridges 2004).

## ⟳ Reflection on the end of coaching

» What's different now that the coaching comes to a close?
» Who are you now, as a result of the work you've put into the coaching?
» What do you believe about yourself and your capacity to think and create change?
» What will you miss once we close our coaching together?
» How are you feeling?
» What can you reclaim to balance what you'll miss?
» What's over? What's not over?
» What can you pack away in a metaphorical suitcase to place on top of the wardrobe for future use, even though it may not be needed right now?
» What can you not take with you, and what don't you want to keep for another time?
» What do you assume that you need to let go of? Is that assumption correct?
» What will you take with you from this coaching on your journey to the future?
» What do you gain by travelling to this new future?
» What's the value to you of this new future?
» What do you need or want to celebrate this ending?
» How would you like to mark the ending?
» How do you want to say goodbye?
» What are you thankful for? How will you articulate that?
» If you were to put a title to the chapter of this coaching that's drawing to a close, what would it be?

And what of the new beginning? What questions might be useful to set them up for success as they embark on this next chapter?

- » What's the title of this next chapter?
- » What are your priorities, goals or intentions for this next chapter?
- » Who do you wish to continue to become?
- » What do you wish to continue learning?
- » What personal strengths can you draw on?
- » Who's now in your personal support group that you'll continue to lean on?
- » Who else might you need to surround yourself with for this new chapter?
- » What other external resources can you draw on?
- » How and when will you give yourself space and time to reflect and strategise?
- » What final words of wisdom would you like to give to yourself as you embark on this new phase?

Some thinkers (and coaches too, come to that) have difficulties with endings, perhaps due to unhappy endings in previous life experiences. Some even defer their last session because they don't want the ickiness of ending or want to keep something in their back pocket for later – or they may simply disappear without a proper ending.

**It's important to make this a good ending, to model what that can be like, even where the thinker has experienced bad endings in the past.**

You may use the ending to consider the thinker's relationship to endings in general if that's useful to them:

* What's your pattern of endings?
* What can we learn together here in this ending about what makes a good ending?
* What beginnings are there for you in this ending?
* How would you like this coaching to end for you to feel complete?

But if they keep deferring or even go AWOL, you can still do that for yourself as coach for your own sense of completion. This is one important piece of processing that you can take to supervision.

For more on endings, see Shifts 17 and 79 in *The Transformational Coach*.

# Summary

When we close a coaching programme, the thinker will continue their progress. They don't stop just because you're no longer in their life – that would be infantilising for you to even think that. But they're not alone. By this time, you'll have supported them to identify their own board of directors or accountability buddies, people they can rely on when you're no longer in the picture. You'll have worked with them to ask for what they need from whomever they need it. That may still be a work in progress, but it's progress they can make if we and they believe in their capacity to do so. Believe!

## Reflective practice

* What do *you* believe about the closing session in relation to agency?
* Which of your values are showing up (or even being triggered) as you read this chapter? What does that tell you?
* What will you ask for and from whom? Which of these boundaries are non-negotiable and in which circumstances might you flex?
* What's the one thing you'll commit to experiment with that will make a marginal gain in the agency of the people with whom you work?

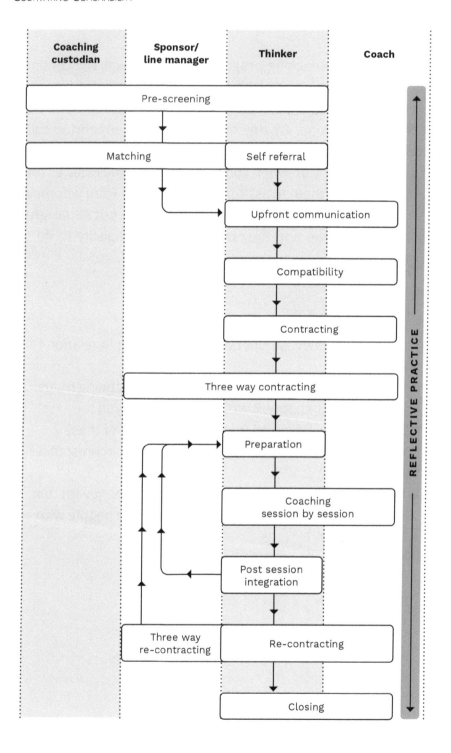

# Chapter 15

# The thinker experience in summary

You've now had the complete chronology of the thinker experience and the touchpoints for screening for and enhancing coaching readiness and agency.

What do you know now about coaching readiness, coachability and agency that you didn't know at the start of this book? With that new knowledge, what are your next steps? How will you hold yourself accountable to those experiments? What inner resources can you draw on? What support might you call on?

Opposite is a reminder of the experience that we've covered, in pictorial form. How might you make this process of developing agency your own?

You may still be left thinking about situations where you're working with established leaders, who feel that through coaching they are outgrowing their own leaders. They're finding their own voice and want to change the culture of the organisation such that everyone across the organisation can also find their own voice through coaching. That could be another whole book in its own right, supporting a culture change in the organisation through the people with whom you work. I'll leave that book to someone else! But if it's a situation you're facing and you haven't found answers here, or if you have other questions that have percolated to the surface for you, given the unique set of thinkers and systems with whom you work, that's what supervision is for.

# Chapter 16

# Reflective practice through a coachability lens

If you're feeling any pain points around aspects of this book, I hope that my reflections will have prompted new insights for you and new questions to ask of yourself, given your context, beliefs and values around coaching readiness, coachability and agency.

I hope you've been reflecting as you've moved through each chapter. If not, I encourage you to re-read each chapter and make personalised commitments to experiment, no matter how small each test might be. Small changes can make a big difference, each as a standalone, marginal gain and also cumulatively. Maybe get together with other coaches who have read this book to support each other in putting new processes in place.

**Don't think you have to be strong and go it alone.** Think about how you build your own agency. Just because I've offered structures, templates and questions doesn't make these the only way; find your own way, your own self-efficacy, building on your signature strengths.

If you're left with more questions than answers, these might be perfect candidates to take to supervision and ponder aloud, either one to one or in a group. You won't be the only one asking yourself these questions, and this is where group supervision can normalise your experiences and then stretch you into new ways of being.

You can find out more about my supervision offerings at **clarenormancoachingassociates.com**

Many other supervisors are available and you can find them through your own coaching body.

## Reflective practice

❋ What questions has this book prompted but not answered?

❋ With whom will you discuss those questions to gain further insights for your own practice?

# Acknowledgements

Every person in my network, past and present, has contributed in some way to the person I am today, the experience and knowledge I possess and the books and articles I've written. I would like to acknowledge every single one of them, but as there are thousands, that wouldn't make for great reading.

So I simply say, if our paths have crossed, thank you – no matter what your role, for whatever you brought to our relationship and my growth. Sometimes it's impossible to tell where a thought or a piece of wisdom came from after it has been in the mix with so many other thoughts and pieces of wisdom from other relationships and become a part of who I am and what I believe. But if we've had any exchange at all, you planted at least one of the seeds that's now blossoming in this book and in my wider work.

Also thanks to all of the authors and researchers whose writing I've consumed and cogitated over; and, come to that, any creator of words or experiences. I make meaning from all sorts of weird and wonderful things around me. We may never have met, but there are always seeds of ideas that flower into some new hybrid concept or activity for me.

Thanks to the talented publishing team at the Right Book Company for bringing these seeds to the light through this newest offering.

And thank you to those I interviewed for your stories, my early reviewers for your honest feedback, and anyone else who gave input.

I will mention one person by name. Sam Humphrey: thank you for your provocations as we co-wrote the sections about coaching in organisations. Two heads and hearts were definitely better than this one alone.

Sending love out to anyone who is 'meeting' me here in this book for the first time. I acknowledge you for making this one of the seeds in your own uniquely shaped wisdom.

# Appendix

## ☉ Thinker readiness

Rate yourself on a scale of 0–5, for each of these mindsets, where:

0 = I'm not at all in alignment with this mindset

5 = I'm completely in alignment with this mindset.

**Your mindset for coaching**: rate yourself 0–5 for each mindset.

✳ I commit to deep thinking, to make sense of the situation, my thoughts and feelings.

✳ I'm willing to think about things in new ways.

✳ I'm willing to use my head, heart and gut to access new thinking.

✳ I realise that there's no one right answer for the issues I bring to coaching – only answers that fit my unique needs, personality and context.

✳ I understand that meaningful change happens when I focus on who I wish to be, not just the problems I need to solve.

✳ I'm willing to experiment in coaching and outside of it.

✳ I believe in my capacity to be resourceful as I make changes.

**Your readiness for coaching**: rate yourself 0–5 for each mindset.

✳ I'm ready to introduce change into my life.

✳ I'm choosing coaching rather than being told to have coaching.

✳ I understand that coaching isn't mentoring, teaching or consulting – and won't try to hook my coach into those modalities.

✳ I'll identify what matters most to me to work on in coaching.

✳ I'll bring my whole self to coaching – vulnerabilities, emotions and all.

✳ I'm ready to be challenged.

✳ I realise that we can only work on me in coaching, not other people.

✳ I'll look for possibilities vs impossibilities.

**Thinking accelerators**: rate yourself 0–5 for each mindset.

✳ I get enough sleep to enable me to think clearly.

✳ The level of my physical activity promotes my mental acuity.

✳ I take myself to a green space at least once a day to restore my attention (whether a forest, a park, a common, a scrap of land at the end of my street).

✳ My diet supports critical thinking.

✳ I drink enough water to keep my brain hydrated and at peak thinking capacity.

✳ I proactively keep my stress levels under control.

✳ I'm purposeful in my use of technology so as not to drain my energy.

**Logistics**: rate yourself 0–5 for each mindset.

✳ I commit to blocking time before a coaching session to prepare mentally.

✳ I commit to blocking time before a coaching session to prepare my body (rehydrating, feeding my brain and using the bathroom).

✳ I commit to blocking time after a coaching session to reflect.

✳ I commit to turning up on time, every time.

✳ I commit to switching off distractions during the coaching session.

✳ I commit to carving out deep thinking time in my diary, over and above my coaching.

If you've rated yourself at 0 for most of the mindsets, coaching probably won't work for you until and unless you're willing to shift your mindset.

If you've rated yourself a 4 or 5 for most of the mindsets, you're likely to be very coachable.

Now that you've rated yourself on each of these mindsets, take some time to think about how you might shift your rating upwards in order to get more out of the coaching process – if you choose to, of course.

* How will you shift your mindsets?
* How might your coach support you with those shifts?
* What do you want to do differently before, during and after coaching, to ensure that you wring the most value from this experience?

# Bibliography

Amabile, T & Kramer, S (2011) *The Progress Principle: Using small wins to ignite joy, engagement, and creativity at work*. Harvard Business Review Press.

Anagnostakis, A (2023) 'Is giving advice helping others' vertical development or stealing their learning?'. URL: verticaldevelopment.education/p/is-giving-advice-helping-others-vertical-development-or-stealing-their-learning

Asay, T P & Lambert, M J (1999) 'The empirical case for the common factors in therapy: Quantitative findings'. In Hubble, M A, Duncan, BL & Miller, S D (eds), *The Heart and Soul of Change: What works in therapy*. American Psychological Association.

Bacon, T & Pool, A (2003) 'Can coaching effectiveness be measured?' Lore International Institute. URL: teamandgroupcoachacademy.com/wp-content/uploads/2017/09/025CanCoachingEffectivenessBeMeasuredBacon.pdf

Bandura, A (2006) 'Toward a psychology of human agency'. *Perspectives on Psychological Science* 1(2). URL: doi.org/10.1111/j.1745-6916.2006.00011.x

Bartolome, G, Vila, S et al (2022) 'Right cortical activation during generation of creative insights: an electroencephalographic study of coaching'. *Frontiers in Education* 7. URL: doi.org/10.3389/feduc.2022.753710

Beck, A T (1972). *Depression: Causes and Treatment*. University of Pennsylvania Press.

Bentler, P M & Speckart, G (1981) 'Attitudes "cause" behaviors: A structural equation analysis'. *Journal of Personality and Social Psychology*. URL: psycnet.apa.org/record/1981-32837-001

Berne, E (1964) *Games People Play*. Grove Press.

Berry, R M, Ashby, J S et al (2011) 'A comparison of face-to-face and distance coaching practices: Coaches' perceptions of the role of working alliance in problem resolution'. *Consulting*

*Psychology Journal: Practice and Research*. URL: dx.doi.
org/10.1037/a0026735

Biswas-Diener, R (2023) *Positive Provocation: 25 questions to elevate your coaching practice*. Berrett-Koehler Publishers.

Bridges, W (2004) *Transitions: Making sense of life's changes*. Da Capo Press.

Brown, P C, Roediger, H L III & McDaniel, M A (2014) *Make it Stick: The science of successful learning*. Belknap Press.

Cavanaugh, K et al (2021) 'On coachability: How practitioners determine whether someone can be coached'. *The International Journal of Mentoring and Coaching* XIII. URL: emccglobal.org/journal_library/volume-xiii-volume-1-july-2021

Chao, L P, Tumer, I & Ishii, K (2005) 'Design process error-proofing: Benchmarking gate and phased review life-cycle models'. *Proceedings of the ASME Design Engineering Technical Conference*. URL: computationalnonlinear.asmedigitalcollection.asme.org/IDETC-CIE/proceedings-abstract/IDETC-CIE2005/47411b/301/313016

Clance, P & Imes, S (1978) 'The Impostor phenomenon in high achieving women: dynamics and therapeutic intervention'. *Psychotherapy: Theory, Research & Practice.* URL: psycnet.apa.org/doiLanding?doi=10.1037%2Fh0086006

Clutterbuck, D (2020) *The Leader's Guide to Being Coached: A practical guide*. Wordscape Ltd.

Clutterbuck, D (2022) *Coaching and Mentoring: A journey through the models, theories, frameworks and narratives of David Clutterbuck*. Routledge.

Covey, S (1999) *The 7 Habits of Highly Effective People*. Simon & Schuster.

Craig, S D (2012) 'Confusion's Impact on Learning'. In: Seel, N M (ed) *Encyclopaedia of the Sciences of Learning*. Springer. URL: doi.org/10.1007/978-1-4419-1428-6_999

De Haan, E & Nilsson, V O (2023) 'What can we know about the effectiveness of coaching? A meta-analysis based only on randomized controlled trials'. Academy of Management

Learning and Education. URL: journals.aom.org/doi/10.5465/amle.2022.0107

De Haan, E (2008) *Relational Coaching: Journeys towards mastering one-to-one learning*. Wiley Publishing.

Dean, K & Humphrey, S (2019) *Coaching Stories: Flowing and falling of being a coach.* Routledge.

Drake, D B (2023) 'The Integrative Assessment Framework: a new paradigm for the development of coaches'. Institute of Coaching/The Moment Institute. URL: instituteofcoaching.org/resourcefile/five-maturities-new-paradigm-developing-coaches-2nd-edition/24038

Dweck, C (2017) *Mindset: Changing the way you think to fulfil your potential*, 6th edition. Random House Publishing.

Eisenstein, C (2018) URL: charleseisenstein.org/courses/living-in-the-gift

Eliot, T S (1942) 'Little Gidding', *Four Quartets*. New English Weekly.

Ellis, Albert (1957) 'Rational psychotherapy and individual psychology'. *Journal of Individual Psychology*. URL: psycnet.apa.org/record/1958-05549-001

Gottlieb, L (2024) featured as a guest on Steven Bartlett's *The Diary of a CEO* podcast. URL: youtu.be/q6hbUZL0fgl?si=krnBnWEFznx-T_-c

Green, L S, Oades, L G & Grant, A M (2007) 'Cognitive-behavioral, solution-focused life coaching: Enhancing goal striving, well-being, and hope'. *Journal of Positive Psychology*, 18 February. URL: doi.org/10.1080/17439760600619849

Hanson, R (2013) *Hardwiring Happiness: The new brain science of contentment, calm, and confidence*. Harmony Books.

Hastings, J V (2021) *Coaching from the Inside: The guiding principles of internal coaching.* Open University Press.

Hawkins, P & Turner, E (2020) *Systemic Coaching: Delivering value beyond the individual.* Routledge.

Heath, C & Heath, D (2017) *The Power of Moments.* Bantam Press.

Heffernan, M (2020) *Uncharted: How to map the future together*. Simon & Schuster UK.

Hogan Assessment Systems, Inc (2017). URL: hoganassessments.com

Hullinger, A M & DiGirolamo, J A (2018) 'Referring a client to therapy: A set of guidelines'. International Coaching Federation. URL: coachingfederation.org/client-referral-whitepaper

Kaplan, S (1995) 'The restorative benefits of nature: toward an integrative framework'. *Journal of Environmental Psychology*. URL: psycnet.apa.org/record/1996-18636-001

Kline, N (2002) *Time to Think: Listening to ignite the human mind*. Cassell.

Koch, D A (2024) 'Principles to make learning brain-friendly'. Association of Talent Development. URL: td.org/product/p/252404

Koch, D A & Gittleson, J (2013) 'High Performance Learners' presentation at Maisie conference.

Krznaric R (2021) *The Good Ancestor: How to think long term in a short-term world*. WH Allen.

Leonard, G (1991) *Mastery: The keys to success and long-term fulfilment*. Penguin.

Locke, E A & Latham, G P (2012) *New Developments in Goal Setting and Task Performance*. Routledge.

LUMA Institute (2012) *Innovating for People: The handbook of human-centered design methods*. URL: luma-institute.com/wp-content/uploads/2021/02/22Innovating-for-People22-Looking.pdf

Marx, M J (2018) 'When the client is thinking of suicide'. URL: coachingfederation.org/blog/when-the-client-is-thinking-of-suicide

McKenna, D & Davis, S L (2009) 'Hidden in plain sight: The active ingredients of executive coaching'. *Industrial and Organizational Psychology*. URL: researchgate.net/publication/253248130_Hidden_in_Plain_Sight_The_Active_Ingredients_of_Executive_Coaching

Menaul, J (2024) URL: youtube.com/channel/

UCy8XgC9uyPqYgaBiMax5PnA/about

Mosconi, L (2019) *Brain Food: How to eat smart and sharpen your mind*. Penguin Life.

Mosley, M (2023) *4 Weeks to Better Sleep: A life-changing plan for deep sleep, improved brain function and feeling great*. Short Books.

Norman C and Ridgley S (2021) 'Lifting the lid on coaching supervision'. Lifting the Lid, episode 36 (with Peter Hawkins). URL: spreaker.com/episode/lifting-the-lid-episode-36-the-one-where-we-talk-about-bigger-things-than-the-individual-with-peter-hawkins--44869882

Norman, C (2022) *The Transformational Coach*. Right Book Press.

Osman, S, Lane, J & Goldsmith, M (2023) *Becoming Coachable: Unleashing the power of executive coaching to transform your leadership and life*. 100 Coaches.

Ouellette, J A & Wood, W (1998) 'Habit and intention in everyday life: The multiple processes by which past behavior predicts future behavior'. *Psychological Bulletin*. URL: psycnet.apa.org/record/1998-04232-003

Peter, L J and Hull, R (1969). *The Peter Principle*. William Morrow & Co Inc.

Prochaska, J O, Norcross, J & DiClemente, C (1994) *Changing for Good: A revolutionary six-stage program for overcoming bad habits and moving your life positively forward*. Avon Books.

Reis, H T (2007) 'Steps towards the ripening of relationship science'. *Personal Relationships* 14. URL: onlinelibrary.wiley.com/doi/abs/10.1111/j.1475-6811.2006.00139.x

Rock, D & Schwartz, J (2006) 'The neuroscience of leadership: Breakthroughs in brain research explain how to make organizational transformation succeed'. *Strategy + Business*, 30 May. URL: strategy-business.com/article/06207

Rogers, T H J (2022) via a LinkedIn exchange of ideas. URL: thinkingfeelingbeing.com

Rosenberg, M B (2003) *Non-violent Communication*. Puddle Dancer Press.

Snyder, C R, Lopez, S J & Edwards, L M (2021) *The Oxford*

*Handbook of Positive Psychology*. Oxford University Press.

Van Tulleken, C (2023) *Ultra-Processed People: Why do we all eat stuff that isn't food... and why can't we stop?* Cornerstone Press.

Whitworth, L, Kimsey-House, H & Sandahl, P (1998) *Co-active Coaching*. Davies Black Publishing.

Woudstra, G (2021) *Mastering the Art of Team Coaching*. Right Book Press.

Zander R & Zander B (2000) *The Art of Possibility: Transforming professional and personal life*. Harvard Business Review Press.

## Online resources

Norman, C & Ridgley, *Lifting the Lid on Coaching Supervision* podcast available at:

* ✳ Apple: podcasts.apple.com/gb/podcast/lifting-the-lid-on-coaching-supervision/id1533533535
* ✳ Spotify: open.spotify.com/show/6okbc7fiaX5UNsl92ZQHR0
* ✳ Amazon/Audible: amazon.co.uk/Lifting-Lid-Coaching-Supervision/dp/B0D4DS1CR7

The Burke Litwin Change Model: mindtools.com/auj0r0y/the-burke-litwin-change-model

Coaching infrastructure audit: grit.co.uk

Hub of Hope: hubofhope.co.uk

ICF PCC Markers: coachingfederation.org/credentials-and-standards/performance-evaluations/pcc-markers

McKinsey 7-S: mckinsey.com/capabilities/strategy-and-corporate-finance/our-insights/enduring-ideas-the-7-s-framework

Mind: mind.org.uk

PESTLE analysis: cipd.org/uk/knowledge/factsheets/pestle-analysis-factsheet

SWOT analysis: cipd.org/uk/knowledge/factsheets/swot-analysis-factsheet

Many resources, checklists, questionnaires and templates are available on my website. Please feel free to steal these with pride, but adapt them to match your style, beliefs, values and motivations. If you would like editable versions of these resources, scan the QR code below or download them at **clarenormancoachingassociates.com/cultivating-coachability/templates** and use the code **ValueCreation**.

*Also by Clare Norman*

# The Transformational Coach

Right Book Press 2022 • ISBN 9781912300822

Do you ever doubt your coaching style is achieving the best results for your clients? Have you ever felt there's room for growth, but you're not sure how to achieve it?

To create a more sustainable transformation in the people you coach, you need to start with your own mindset. As a coach, you know you can't change what you do unless you alter what you believe first.

By shedding the ineffective scripts, trappings and beliefs that a lifetime of personal interactions, professional training and even your parents have taught you, you can reset your thinking to a beginner's mentality and so begin a fulfilling and exciting journey to coaching mastery.

In this fresh and highly effective field guide, Master Mentor Coach Clare Norman gets into your head to help you pinpoint the attitudes that you need to unlearn and reframe.

Through Clare's rich experience, illuminating real-life stories, and practical guidance you can shift towards more useful thinking and powerful skillsets by spotting and changing your own restrictive coaching mindsets.

It's time to ditch the old beliefs that are holding you back, free your thinking and make the move from getting transactional results to being a transformational coach.

*Also by Clare Norman*

# Mentor Coaching: A Practical Guide

McGraw Hill 2020 • ISBN 9780335248797

This practical guide argues that both mentor coaching and supervision be mandated by the professional coaching bodies as part of coaches' continuous professional development.

Mentor coaching is not just for those coaches seeking a credential: it is for lifelong professional development for every coach, at every level of the profession. You are the best coaching tool there is. Tools need to be oiled, sharpened, repaired and protected to keep them in tip-top condition. That's what mentor coaching and supervision do – they keep coaches sharp and fit for purpose.

The reader will learn how to develop as a coach using mentor coaching, as well as how to develop as a mentor coach, to support other coaches to develop. Clare Norman explains what mentor coaching is, why it is so important and the competencies for mentor coaching. How coaches show up in the room is more important than how much we know about the theory behind coaching.

Clare Norman's concise book is important reading for all practising coaches, as well as coaches and mentor coaches in training.